Consumerism

Other Books of Related Interest:

Opposing Viewpoints Series

Government Spending

Poverty

Current Controversies

Developing Nations

Globalization

At Issue Series

What Is the Future of the U.S. Economy?

Consumerism

Uma Kukathas, Book Editor

GREENHAVEN PRESS
A part of Gale, Cengage Learning

Detroit • New York • San Francisco • New Haven, Conn • Waterville, Maine • London

Christine Nasso, *Publisher*
Elizabeth Des Chenes, *Managing Editor*

© 2008 Greenhaven Press, a part of Gale, Cengage Learning.

For more information, contact:
Greenhaven Press
27500 Drake Rd.
Farmington Hills, MI 48331-3535
Or you can visit our Internet site at gale.cengage.com

For product information and technology assistance, contact us at

Gale Customer Support, 1-800-877-4253
For permission to use material from this text or product, submit all requests online at www.cengage.com/permissions

Further permissions questions can be emailed to permissionrequest@cengage.com

Articles in Greenhaven Press anthologies are often edited for length to meet page requirements. In addition, original titles of these works are changed to clearly present the main thesis and to explicitly indicate the author's opinion. Every effort is made to ensure that Greenhaven Press accurately reflects the original intent of the authors. Every effort has been made to trace the owners of copyrighted material.

Cover photograph reproduced by permission of photos.com.

LIBRARY OF CONGRESS CATALOGING-IN-PUBLICATION DATA

Consumerism / Uma Kukathas, book editor.
    p. cm. -- (Contemporary issues companion)
  Includes bibliographical references and index.
  ISBN-13: 978-0-7377-3956-5 (hardcover)
  ISBN-13: 978-0-7377-3957-2 (pbk.)
  1. Consumption (Economics). 2. Consumption (Economics)--Environmental aspects.
3. Consumer behavior. I. Kukathas, Uma.
  HC79.C6C657 2008
  339.4'7--dc22
                                                                    2008006569

Printed in the United States of America
   1 2 3 4 5   12 11 10 09 08

ED225

Contents

Foreword

In the news, on the streets, and in neighborhoods, individuals are confronted with a variety of social problems. Such problems may affect people directly: A young woman may struggle with depression, suspect a friend of having bulimia, or watch a loved one battle cancer. And even the issues that do not directly affect her private life—such as religious cults, domestic violence, or legalized gambling—still impact the larger society in which she lives. Discovering and analyzing the complexities of issues that encompass communal and societal realms as well as the world of personal experience is a valuable educational goal in the modern world.

Effectively addressing social problems requires familiarity with a constantly changing stream of data. Becoming well informed about today's controversies is an intricate process that often involves reading myriad primary and secondary sources, analyzing political debates, weighing various experts' opinions—even listening to firsthand accounts of those directly affected by the issue. For students and general observers, this can be a daunting task because of the sheer volume of information available in books, periodicals, on the evening news, and on the Internet. Researching the consequences of legalized gambling, for example, might entail sifting through congressional testimony on gambling's societal effects, examining private studies on Indian gaming, perusing numerous Web sites devoted to Internet betting, and reading essays written by lottery winners as well as interviews with recovering compulsive gamblers. Obtaining valuable information can be time-consuming—since it often requires researchers to pore over numerous documents and commentaries before discovering a source relevant to their particular investigation.

Greenhaven's Contemporary Issues Companion series seeks to assist this process of research by providing readers with useful and pertinent information about today's complex issues. Each volume in this anthology series focuses on a topic of current interest, presenting informative and thought-provoking selections written from a wide variety of viewpoints. The readings selected by the editors include such diverse sources as personal accounts and case studies, pertinent factual and statistical articles, and relevant commentaries and overviews. This diversity of sources and views, found in every Contemporary Issues Companion, offers readers a broad perspective in one convenient volume.

In addition, each title in the Contemporary Issues Companion series is designed especially for young adults. The selections included in every volume are chosen for their accessibility and are expertly edited in consideration of both the reading and comprehension levels of the audience. The structure of the anthologies also enhances accessibility. An introductory essay places each issue in context and provides helpful facts such as historical background or current statistics and legislation that pertain to the topic. The chapters that follow organize the material and focus on specific aspects of the book's topic. Every essay is introduced by a brief summary of its main points and biographical information about the author. These summaries aid in comprehension and can also serve to direct readers to material of immediate interest and need. Finally, a comprehensive index allows readers to efficiently scan and locate content.

The Contemporary Issues Companion series is an ideal launching point for research on a particular topic. Each anthology in the series is composed of readings taken from an extensive gamut of resources, including periodicals, newspapers, books, government documents, the publications of private and public organizations, and Internet Web sites. In these volumes, readers will find factual support suitable for use in reports, debates, speeches, and research papers. The anthologies also facilitate further research, featuring a book and periodical bibliography and a list of organizations to contact for additional information.

A perfect resource for both students and the general reader, Greenhaven's Contemporary Issues Companion series is sure to be a valued source of current, readable information on social problems that interest young adults. It is the editors' hope that readers will find the Contemporary Issues Companion series useful as a starting point to formulate their own opinions about and answers to the complex issues of the present day.

Introduction

On June 29, 2007, in cities across the United States, from New York to San Francisco, groups of people—sometimes in the hundreds—were seen gathered on sidewalks in downtown business districts, forming lines that wrapped around several blocks. Some had camped overnight; a few were reported to have been there for three days, enduring thunderstorms and rain. Who were these faithful, and who, or what, were they anticipating? They were not striking workers demanding better wages or labor conditions. They were not religious devotees awaiting their spiritual leader. Neither were they angered citizens demonstrating against the war in Iraq, then in its fourth year.

The several thousand waiting in line in cities all over the country were neither pilgrims nor protesters—they were shoppers. These intrepid sale-seekers, many in sleeping bags and tents, were not waiting outside churches or federal buildings, but outside Apple stores for their shot at being the first to buy the iPhone, the technology company's hottest new gadget—a cellular phone with computing and Wi-Fi capabilities. These die-hard consumers admitted in interviews that they simply had to have the product, and have it now. Some hired others to wait in line for them while they attended meetings or work—or took a bathroom break. Philadelphia mayor John Street, a self-proclaimed "gadget guy," was among them. "This is the latest," he declared, "and I'm going to have it."

The hype for the phone began six months earlier, when Apple began to release tidbits of information to the public about the device's capabilities. Before long, the iPhone had become one of the most desired new products in the United States. In the six months prior to its release, it was the subject of eleven thousand print articles and 69 million searches on Google. While the frenzy surrounding the iPhone was out of control, by all accounts, it pointed to what had become a recognizable trend in American contemporary culture. A new "must-have" object had become big news in the media, igniting a passionate desire among consumers to compete for ownership of it.

The desire for material possessions is nothing new, of course; the lust for gold and possessions has been a constant in human history. But, several scholars have argued, with the rise of capitalism and the resulting increase in global trade over the last five hundred years, the idea of acquisition as a basic human good has taken firm root, particularly in Western societies—something displayed dramatically in the mad clamoring for a computer manufacturer's latest toy. The historian Peter Stearns in his book *Consumerism and World History* argues further that in the last century the pace of acquisition has quickened to such a degree that the world today is "permeated by consumerism." There is disagreement among scholars as to exactly how to define "consumerism," but there is some consensus that it is the equating of well-being with the purchase and consumption of material possessions. Some commentators have identified modern society as a consumer society because consumption has become the principal aspiration, source of identity, and leisure activity for its members. They say that in the last sixty years, the focus of human life, especially in the West, has changed so that people no longer consume to live, but formulate their goals in life through acquiring goods that they clearly do not need for subsistence.

For many American consumers, the acquisition of a new iPhone did indeed become an important aspiration and goal. The fervor it stirred up, including heated discussions on blogs regarding its features and value (supporters dubbed it the "Jesus phone," and referred to its launch as iDay; decriers spent endless hours lambasting it), made it clear that for some consumers the item was inextricably linked with their identity. Apple cultists, as they called themselves, acknowledged that the phone was little more useful than the phones they already owned, and not an essential business device, but they wanted one nonetheless because of its superior technology, aesthetic appeal, and "cool" factor. The high cost of the phone ($499 to $599), plus the cost of a two-year wireless plan at $60 a month with exclusive carrier AT&T, was no deterrent either.

For many critics, the reaction to and interest in the iPhone among consumers is indicative of how American society is being transformed on a number of levels as consumerism takes the place of religion, family, and society. The philosopher Julian Baggini remarks on this trend, suggesting that consumerism has supplanted the need for the spiritual; like religion, he says, shopping promises comfort and relief from suffering. The sociologist Zygmunt Bauman argues that consumerism has impacted social identities and societal behavior by changing the traditional relationship between needs and satisfaction and by promoting aesthetic interests above ethical ones. No longer is moral improvement an important driving force in social behavior, but rather the aesthetic appreciation of a "cool" object that will somehow confer meaning and joy to one's life. Benjamin R. Barber of the University of Maryland similarly contends that consumer culture in the United States has created a society of perennial adolescents who drive the economy but take little responsibility for more important life concerns.

According to Juliet B. Schor, an economist and professor of sociology at Boston University, the modern culture of consumption has taken root because of a number of sociological factors. After the Second World War, she maintains, the frames of reference for most Americans shifted from their families and neighborhoods to the upper middle class and the rich seen portrayed on television and in advertisements. The need to "keep up" with the perceived wealth of others, the "upscaling in people's sense of need," moved Americans to want to acquire more and more—including larger houses, bigger cars, and a host of disposable goods. In the early years of the twenty-first century, those goods are, increasingly, devices using the newest technology—the thinnest computer, the largest and clearest television screen, the sleekest telephone.

While critics of consumerism have written extensively about the negative effects of consumerism on American children and adults, they point out, too, that the impact of Americans' consumption is far more wide-reaching. The rampant consumerism of the developed world, they say, is the driving force behind the dire poverty that affects more than 3 billion people on the planet, and it is the moral responsibility of those who use so much of the world's resources to redress that imbalance. Wendell Berry and other environmentalists argue similarly that the current rate of consumption among Westerners is unsustainable. Berry also laments the fact that Americans have allowed corporate interests to destroy land in the name of "freedom" and "growth," when this has not ultimately benefited the people or land at all.

Apple, like many large corporations, is aware of the criticisms that have been leveled at them by anticonsumerism advocates in general and environmentalists in particular. In May 2007, just before the launch of the iPhone, CEO Steve Jobs made a commitment to a "Greener Apple," pledging to produce products that had less harmful impact on the Earth. However, later that year, Greenpeace released a study and report charging that the iPhone contained hazardous chemicals and materials, a charge that the company firmly denied. Nonprofit groups have also pointed out that the young Chinese migrant laborers assembling iPhones earn around fifty dollars a month, a tenth of the cost of the device. However, Apple has replied that the manufacturing is done in accordance with existing labor laws, and that the buying power of those wages was significant.

Like consumerism in general, the Apple iPhone has come under fire from a number of quarters. For some anticonsumerists, the phone has become a symbol of technology that has been used unwisely, harnessed to serve the childish needs of the idle rich. It has become a sign for what Americans erroneously place value on, and how their needs and wants have become conflated. From its manufacturing to its marketing, the phone has been viewed as misusing precious environmental resources and drawing large profits at the expense of workers and American consumers.

However, for those very consumers, none of this seems to matter very much at all. In the first weekend after hitting shelves, the iPhone sold over five hundred thousand units. A controversy erupted when the company dropped the price by two hundred dollars just months after the initial launch, but it did little to dampen enthusiasm for the product; by year's end, more than 5 million customers had purchased the phone. The fervent dedication to the product has not diminished, and it continues to garner rave reviews throughout the industry as a revolution in mobile computing. According to most media analysts, the iPhone has lived up to its hype and more. In a consumer survey, it was found that 32 percent of Americans who do not currently own an iPhone intend to purchase one. This makes the iPhone the most successful product introduction of the twenty-first century, and one that could radically transform the consumer purchasing experience and shape the future of consumerism.

CHAPTER 1

Consumerism
and Society

The Development of Consumerism

Peter N. Stearns

Peter N. Stearns is provost and professor of history at George Mason University in Virginia. In the following article, he traces the development of consumerism and says it has profoundly altered human behavior and personal expectations; in the last century it has made people define life differently than at any other time in history. He explains that consumerism has developed and continues to flourish because of a number of factors, including manipulation, fulfillment of social and personal needs, and habituation. Stearns also discusses three issues surrounding consumerism's future: the tensions between religion and consumerism, the social protests against multinational corporations and global trade policies, and the growing economic gap worldwide.

History answers several basic questions about consumerism—for example, why did it get started, and how do different societies vary? It defines other questions that require more personal evaluation. . . .

The development of consumerism represents one of the great changes in the human experience, literally around the world, over the past two or three centuries. The emergence of new types of marketing and advertising is important in itself, as part of modern economic history. But it is the shift in behavior and personal expectations that is really intriguing. Large numbers of people have come to define life somewhat differently, and have fostered new kinds of hopes and frustrations accordingly.

This is a recent development, as big historical shifts go, but already it has a complex history. Far more is involved than the apparent simplicity of shopping and acquiring.

Peter N. Stearns, *Consumerism in World History: The Global Transformation of Desire*. Second Edition, Andover, Hampshire: Routledge, 2006. Copyright © 2001, 2006 Peter N. Stearns. Reproduced by permission of the publisher.

Historical Factors in the Development of Consumerism

While consumerism shows the power of change—a key focus for historical inquiry—it also shows the importance of historical continuities. Each major society has received and elaborated consumerism a bit differently. Key historical factors involved in this distinctive shaping include prior social structures and their degree of rigidity, and of course gender relationships and assumptions as well. The cultural context is also crucial. Consumerism gains ground more smoothly when the prior culture was heavily secular. But even secular philosophies like Confucianism condition the experience. Government involvement can be critical as well; different political traditions have encouraged different levels of state policy to promote, channel or discourage consumerism. The power of consumerism is obvious. Its appeal has often allowed it to advance despite various political, cultural and social obstacles, but the power does not run roughshod over history, which is why international consumerism is not a uniform product.

History also reminds us of crucial differences in timing. Some societies are "farther along" in consumerism than others, and the differences here may prove durable. The historical record also makes it clear that consumerism never progresses unopposed, and that it may even be slowed or temporarily reversed. At the outset of the twenty-first century, powerful objections to consumerism persist in many parts of the world, and we may see new cases in which the consumer apparatus is rolled back. We will certainly see vigorous debate over the phenomenon almost everywhere, though the specific forms will vary from one society to the next.

The importance of variations in the receptions of consumer behaviors may seem unexpected, for it is tempting to look at consumerism as a uniform phenomenon, some undifferentiated product of Westernization. But the variations are real, and they continue to shape consumerism's prospects.

History also explains why consumerism exists at all, though the balance among factors must still prompt debate. The apparatus is one element from the first: consumerism exists partly because so many clever people promote it, with increasingly sophisticated techniques, but consumerism also exists because it meets other needs. Its role in responding to blurrings of identity is crucial. Consumerism helps people deal with confusions about social status and with challenges to established patterns because of new foreign influence. Consumerism also, relatedly, allows quiet challenges to hierarchy, in terms of social class, gender, even parental authority. It provides some sense of freedom and individual expression, however superficial the outcome. And, particularly outside the West, it offers a sense of belonging to a larger whole, of gaining access to the up-to-date and modern. It compensates for change, and also provokes further change in the interests of apparent personal fulfillment and new forms of identity. Finally, of course, consumerism takes increasing root with time, unless (rarely) it is successfully rolled back by effective opposition. People come to grow up with consumerism from infancy; they assume its logic and normalcy.

The combination of three components—manipulation, fulfillment of social and personal needs, and habituation—serves as consumerism's incubator and ongoing support. Shopping may offer some intrinsic pleasures, but there are reasons for its growing role in human life.

Consumerism's Future

History does not, of course, tell us exactly what comes next, and important issues surround consumerism's future. Three question marks particularly apply to consumerism's prospects as the twenty-first century moves forward. The first involves the impact of the religious revival affecting many regions of the world, from Islam, to a new movement in China derived in part from Buddhism, to the surge of Protestant fundamentalism in Latin America, to the increased popularity of religious commitments in the United States. Religious fervor can of course coexist with consumerism, but there are inevitable tensions. Will religion provide an alternative to consumer interests, and if so where, and to what extent? To what extent do the fervent religions take hold particularly among people—the urban unemployed, for example—left out of consumerist gains, and to what extent do they inhibit consumer interests?

The second issue involves the new surge of protest against multinational corporations and global trade policies. This protest led during the year 2000 to unexpectedly vigorous demonstrations against international economic agencies such as the World Bank, in cities ranging from Seattle to Geneva [Switzerland]. The protest does not focus on consumerism per se, but it does argue that protecting jobs and the environment should take precedence over maximizing consumer gains. It also involves groups that do disavow consumer goals outright, harking back to the alternative spirit of the 1960s. Where will this lead? Is it possible that either local or global protests will displace consumerism?

The third issue, related to both the others, involves the growing economic gap that has opened worldwide between the relatively affluent and the increasingly poor. The gap has widened steadily during the past two decades. It involves certain regions, like much of Africa, in disproportionate poverty, at levels that inhibit consumerism of any sort. It also involves left-out groups even within the United States, that have found their incomes stagnating or falling as income inequality becomes sharper. For the poor, consumerism is not the question; seeking adequate subsistence is. The question haunts a large percentage of people in Africa, South Asia, and elsewhere. It haunts the growing number of children below the poverty line—thirteen million in the year 2000—in the United States. Where will the growing inequality trend lead? Will it generate new forms of protest, or will it simply continue to create a divide, within societies as well as internationally, between those who can and those who cannot significantly participate in modern history's new toys? There is an additional twist. Many poor regions and poor people now provide low-wage labor to make consumer goods for others. Long hours and unsafe conditions add in as well. This includes sweated peasant workers in China, making Christmas ornaments or firecrackers, workers making fashionable sneakers in Vietnam, textile workers in Indonesia or Lesotho. Spreading consumerism, and the quest for low prices and greater profits, in this sense contributes directly to poverty, to the great divide between those involved in the system and those left out.

Impact and Meaning of Consumerism

Again, it is essential to assume debate and constraints when contemplating consumerism's future prospects. Some issues are new—environmentalism, for example, at its current level of concern—but complexity has long been part of consumerism's impact.

Still, for all the question marks, it is logical to assume that consumerism will continue to gain ground, as more societies seek to share in the presumed delights. China, for example, clearly seems poised for greater consumerism, and Russian interest is obvious though clouded by uncertain economic prospects. Large middle classes in countries such as India, Mexico, Turkey, and Brazil already define life in part through standard consumer acquisitions. Many other groups and regions seek larger slices of the consumer pie. Even in the United States, amid some questions about whether unprecedented affluence provides enough purpose in life, consumer interests continue to surge forward. Indeed, economies from the United States to China, and to some degree globally, now depend on steady and advancing consumerism. Small wonder that consumer diligence has come to be virtually an obligation of citizenship, particularly in the United States, essential to keep the wheels of society turning. American leaders, urging a return to normalcy after the terrorist attacks of 2001, made the point clearly: "keep buying and keep flying."

The steady intensification of consumerism—despite problems and despite real inequalities—leads to three final questions that focus on evaluation of consumerism's meaning and impact rather than on historical perspective and forecasting alone. First, is consumerism making the world too homogeneous, at undue cost to regional identities and expressions? Second, will the spread of consumerism usher in other historical changes, and of what magnitude? And third, wherever it has hit or will alight, is consumerism a good thing, in terms of human values?

Homogeneity

The homogeneity issue goes to the core of a world-historical approach to consumerism, but it is not easy to deal with. The spread of consumerism does involve convergence on shared goals and many shared styles. To take a simple point: people around the world dress more similarly, at the outset of the twenty-first century, than ever before since clothing was invented.

T-shirts, blue jeans, neckties are everywhere. Consumerism encourages people to seek minor individual variants in clothing—a distinctive slogan on the T-shirt, for example—but amid great, growing, and often truly international conformity.

Indeed, we have seen that one of the goals of consumerism, particularly outside the West, has been a sense of participation in a larger global community. People even accept products they don't greatly like, such as McDonald's fare, in order to gain this sense of belonging, in order to shake off a sense of parochialism and separateness.

Yet homogeneity is far from complete. People continue to differ over consumerism, as a result of the wide disparity in earnings but also because of very different expectations. The

23

rural-urban gap still shows in most societies. Rural people stake more on acquisition of land and family solidarity than their urban cousins do, and work less strenuously to maximize consumer gains. Different societies offer distinctive packages as well. The tensions between consumerism and community traditions in Africa are not felt to the same degree in Japan. Partly this reflects differences in historical timing, but there may be more involved. Japanese consumerism is associated with individualism to a degree, but it has not erased a far greater sense of conformity in Japan than in the West. Europeans spend far more on vacations and vacation time than Americans do, a huge difference in the definitions of appropriate consumerism even within the West. Americans lead the world in personal credit card debt, reflecting a particular addiction to maximizing consumer opportunities as early as possible (or, according to concerned critics, earlier than is really possible). There is no reason to believe that the rest of the world will follow this American example, for again precise goals continue to vary by group and region. Many Indians embrace aspects of consumerism, but they also combine it with local fashions.

In other words, consumerism does erase some divisions and it does create unprecedentedly wide interest in some common types of items, even single brands such as McDonald's or Mickey Mouse or Pokémon. It does permit people to find known consumer emblems virtually everywhere they travel. It does encourage a sense of global belonging. But it does not erase all differences. Whether the world's peoples are becoming too similar around consumerism, or whether too many differences still hamper mutual understanding remains an important tension. Consumerism has not eliminated the tension.

Range of Impact

A second question about consumerism, both past and future, involves range of impact. We have seen that consumerism can affect more than buying habits and personal and family life. Many people believe it has profoundly altered the political process in countries such as the United States, leading to new levels of manipulation in "selling the candidate." But as consumerism deepens, and spreads to still more countries, will there be further effects? One American journalist, Thomas Friedman, in his book *The Lexus and the Olive Tree*, argues that deeply consumerist societies will not wage war against each other. He contends that when lots of people in a society enjoy the fruits of consumerism, they no longer want to go to war, and so war will decline (except, of course, for aggrieved societies where consumerism has not yet taken hold). He notes the unpopularity of military service in many consumerist societies. This is an ambitious theory, and frankly not enough time has passed to judge whether it is right or wrong. (Consumerist England eagerly went to war against Argentina in the 1980s over the Falkland Islands, but of course it was a minor engagement, and also Argentina was not yet fully consumerist, so maybe the theory didn't apply.) But thinking this way about the potential precedent-shattering effects of global consumerism at least points the way to the possibility of wide impacts on our future. The United States attack on Iraq, in 2003, shows that deeply consumerist societies will still go to war when they can be persuaded they are under threat. But the war (like the Vietnam war before it) was also intriguing in that it did not call for significant consumer sacrifice; taxes were not raised and people were encouraged to keep on spending, as government deficits mounted. Perhaps Friedman should be modified: consumerist societies will prefer wars that do not interfere with consumer life, but other goals may take precedence and drive them to battle despite consumerism. And if this is so, how much has this aspect of history really changed?

More basically still: is consumerism "good?" In one sense the question is unanswerable except in terms of personal values, and people clearly disagree. Consumerism can be appallingly shallow. It opens even thoughtful people to manipulations by salesmen and advertisers. It does relate to a decline of spiritual values and other intangibles. It does generate mindless conformities. It may even make people less aware of their own emotional reactions, as they seek to buy yet another item that will distract them. It certainly can reduce protest, making people reluctant to confront social injustice or deteriorations at work so long as their buying power holds up. It can negatively affect the environment, by encouraging unregulated production and creating wasteful products.

But consumerism can be defended, even without denying some of the criticisms. New goods provide new levels of comfort and diversion, and arguably even beauty, into ordinary life. Few people would willingly go back to pre-consumerist material standards—though this may reflect the extent to which consumerism has blinded them to higher values. It is also true that some commentary on consumerism, still today, reflects elitist disdain for the pleasures of the masses and a related sense that the lower orders should not call attention to themselves. It often assumes that ordinary people don't know what's good for them—which is possible but not certain.

It is also vital to recognize how consumerism has often stood for goals and concerns well beyond material acquisition. We have seen that consumerism gives many people a sense of global belonging. It also often stands for freedom and individual choice. This was true in the past and remains true for many today. It often stands as well for an attack on rigid social or gender hierarchy. These strivings through consumerism may be disapproved of, as elite critics have often done when consumer gains challenged hierarchy. Or consumerism may be attacked for serving the goals badly; freedom, for example, may be a goal in consumerism that is thwarted by conformity and commercial manipulation. But a judgment of consumerism must recognize its important service to broader social and personal interests. It is not always as shallow as it seems. Many people express themselves through it, in ways impossible in earlier times.

Loss of Identity

What of the loss of identity consumerism may involve? Consumerism and Westernization are not the same thing, in that some societies, for example those of Japan or Africa, may increase consumerism without totally surrendering to Western values. Outside the West, consumerism has always involved an attack on regional traditions through attraction to imported goods and tastes. This may not only offend nationalist pride, but also seriously disorient individuals who voluntarily commit to consumer goals. They may end up—as some Africans claim to feel—not knowing who they are.

Even in the West, it is hard to say whether consumerism has made people happier. Measuring happiness historically is terribly hard, perhaps impossible. Clearly, the advance of consumerism has always involved losses as well as gains, and some of the drawbacks have not been clearly perceived by enthusiasts. One study, issued in 2000, claims that major consumer gains in a society—a real move upward in material standards—initially causes a definitive jump in measurable happiness. But after that and in more established consumer settings, consumerism is irrelevant to claimed satisfaction, and people enmeshed in milder forms of consumerism may be happier than consumerist zealots.

The study of consumerism in world history does not provide a definitive balance sheet on whether the long-term results are favorable or unfavorable. But it does provide perspective, allowing greater understanding of what consumerism involves, and perspective, in turn, offers a greater capacity to choose an appropriate level of involvement, rather than being swept away by the latest enthusiasm.

Understanding where consumerism comes from, what needs and pressures it responds to, does not prove that consumerism is good or bad. But historical understanding does generate some opportunity for considering one's own take on a truly powerful international force in contemporary life. It also helps to know what some of the criticisms have been, and to be able to compare one set of national patterns against another.

Managing consumerism is a challenge, for it is easy to be managed by it. But consumerism is a human construction, despite all the complex factors behind it. It should serve human ends.

Anticonsumerism Is Not a New Phenomenon

Kim Humphery

Kim Humphery teaches in the School of Social Science and Planning at RMIT University and is conducting an Australian Research Council-funded project on anticonsumerism in the contemporary West. In the following selection, she argues that it has become commonplace for critics of consumption to point to the epidemic of "affluenza." She considers how useful it is to think of consumption as a pathology and says that more useful is the delineation of what overconsumption does socially, personally, and environmentally in the world as it exists today. Modern anticonsumerists often rehash old arguments from previous eras in which consumption was seen as a social ill but without making their arguments compelling for the new sets of problems the world now faces.

The diagnosis is apparently simple, the symptoms often all too clear. If you are a manic shopper, hooked on credit card debt and have a house (and perhaps even a self-storage bay) full of things, then you've probably got it. If you are driven by the chase for social status, overworked, overstressed and perhaps even overweight, then the signs are not good. If you live a life of commodity excess but feel empty inside, if you crave happiness but don't quite have it, then it's almost certain; you've got *affluenza*.

The affluenza virus, or some similar pathology, stands as one of the core concepts within recent discussions of the ills of Western consumer society, from Robert H. Franks' *Luxury Fever* to Tim Kasser's *The High Price of Materialism* to, in Australia, Clive Hamilton's *Growth Fetish*. These and other similar bestsellers have, over the past few years, rejuvenated a much needed public intellectual critique of consumerism, of the Western (and increasingly global) indulgence in the glorious commodities of advanced branded capitalism.

The critique offered within such books, of communities in decay, societies fragmented, individualism lost and nature destroyed is perhaps familiar and open to argument but no less welcome because of this. Familiar too, however, and much more problematic, is the potent mix within many recent books of virology and social critique. Whether conceived as a useful political strategy to get people thinking or as an identifiable condition, talk of affluenza has become the stock-in-trade of the consumer critic. Clearly, recent commentators have seen the language of the virus, the fever, the obsession and the fetish as somehow potentially resonating with those many people within and beyond Western nations now feeling by no means at ease with rampant consumerism.

But just how useful is this language, and the idea of consumption as pathology? What kind of take on society and the individual does all the talk of affluenza actually buy into? And how might we more effectively talk about the major, pressing issue of over-consumption without running to the medical textbook?

The usefulness of pathologising contemporary consumerism—our inordinately high levels of consumption of everything from hold-in-your-hand material things to the 'unseen' commodities of petrol and electricity—is, at best, an open question. A number of commentators talk of affluenza with at least some sense of the dubious, lightweight nature of the concept and with a sense, too, of the dangers of burdening the populace with yet another malady in a world terrified of viruses, both real and virtual.

But other critics of contemporary consumerism are less attuned to irony. Earnestly drawn into their own rhetoric, many a purveyor of the affluenza idea write as if practitioners of evidence-based medicine. Whether attributed to a behaviourist habitualism, a deeply neurotic drive towards emulation, a psychoanalytic sublimation and displacement of true needs or a fundamental spiritual malaise, talk of affluenza can often sink rather rapidly into a pop psychology of the worst order.

Habit, emulation, sublimation, malaise: perhaps all of these are, at various moments, in operation when I wander the mall and stand before a counter. But perhaps not. And it is this perhaps not, this tangled string of triggers and coincidences behind hyperconsumption, which is rarely acknowledged or explored within the new critique of consumerism. Indeed, this is a critique that, while timely and so much needed, can be resolutely static and backward-looking in its relentless deployment of an oversimplified, deterministic model of explaining our present over-consumptive predicament.

No doubt, what drives the use of this simplistic model is the perceived need among many of the new critics of consumerism to lock on to an easily digested, marketable concept that invokes a popular recognition of 'something wrong' and generates media babble. For this, affluenza, in its roll-off-the-tongue way, is a pretty good candidate. Yet, pathologising consumption treads a fine line between resonating with people and turning them away from the very politics and futures you want them to consider. It emulates rather than moves beyond the well-worn and very tired strategies of liberal/radical dissent, and it simulates rather than reinvigorates the old orthodoxies of concerned social commentary.

To take the latter point first: in numerous chance conversations I have had with people about the new critique of consumerism, the complaint is inevitably raised that it is not new, that it is does indeed simply revisit old ideas about consumption as sickness and dropping out as its cure (or 'downshifting' in the latest parlance). In reply, the new critic might answer: 'no, but we are putting the issue of overconsumption back on the agenda'. This is not a bad initial response. But we can take the quibble about newness deeper, and here much of the recent talk of affluenza hits big problems. For what is rekindled within this concept is that nasty little tendency within the social sciences—so well recognised by the philosopher Hannah Arendt back in the mid-twentieth century—towards portraying people as conditioned animals rather than as plural in selfhood and action. This plurality, not individuality, is what allows people to surprise themselves and others; it is, to draw on the work of a more recent philosopher, Elizabeth Grosz, what renders the world and humanity always in process of becoming rather than rigidly patterned.

To put this in less philosophical terms, much of the recent critique of commodity excess works through a strategy of enlightenment proselytism whereby whole populations are seen as conditioned to shop, while the future is being modelled by the unconditioned who have jumped off the treadmill of overwork and overspending. People are thus seen as essentially uniform rather than plural and as divided into two groups, only one of which holds the hope of change and the plan for the future.

Politically, in terms of the long history of oppositional critique, this returns us to the thorny question of false consciousness. And perhaps, in the early twenty-first century, this question might well be opened up once again, at least through recourse to the more sophisticated notion of cultural hegemony. After all, the apparent willingness of most of us, within countries such as Australia, to consume at high levels—or at least desire to do so—and to distance ourselves from the environmental and social costs, does seem to be terribly well explained by the proposition that our consciousness has gone askew.

The problem is that critiques and movements that have utilised this way of thinking have failed dismally in the past to relate to the nuances of everyday life, to get people to think about that life and to bring about change. In short, the pathologising strategy does not have much of a history of intellectual prescience or political success.

By the 1980s, 'false consciousness' had largely disappeared from the left/liberal lexicon, but the idea never really went away. Its full return in the guise of affluenza is thus no surprise. Nor is the fact that it runs into the problems of old. Here, as in all such social diagnostics, the people are both the problem and the hope. They are simultaneously the thing despised, or at best pitied for their spiritless hyperconsumption, and the thing lauded for their banked-on ability to change. Affluenza, the idea, thus delivers a double whammy of retrograde sociology and, sometimes, smug politics: it blithely rekindles the pathology of the purchase and the cherished left/liberal dichotomy between the smart and the dumb, the rational non-consumer and the neuron-free shopper.

The alternative to this simplism, however, is expressly not to run back to a wishy-washy non-judgementalism in which we seek to understand every little subjective complexity and contextualised reason as to why we consume. That would leave us with a bland ethnography of consumption and little structural politics at all. Indeed, few writers now push the shopping as popular resistance line of argument, not least because it has become somewhat dubious to myopically insist that an individual forges an identity, expresses revolt, or gives life to subversive desires through the commodity. Social critique in the age of anti-globalisation has to be more broadly political than this and to consider the impact of consumption beyond the confines of the local and the subjective. But such a broader, renewed politics of consumption might also need to think very seriously about any easy return to strategies of old, and to question the current penchant within recent critiques of consumerism for the medical metaphor.

The real strength of the recently renewed critique of overconsumption does not come from its diagnostics but from its delineation of what overconsumption does, or possibly does, socially, personally and environmentally. Affluenza is doomed to become an honoured member of the pantheon of glib concepts. But, in contrast, the current re-emphasis on the dynamic between nature and industrial culture, production and consumption, and the material and human worlds has real content and a power to mean something to people, to say something that is, if not new, at least about an energetic renewal of oppositional ways of thinking and living. What it renews is a sense that commodities have biographies—from the precious resources used in their production, to the often exploitative work involved in their making, to the logic of profit involved in their selling, to the conflictual meanings surrounding their purchase, to the difficulties plaguing their disposal.

To be sure, many of the solutions offered within recent critiques of Western over-consumption are as underformulated as the flight to pathology. But this does not devalue the essential message conveyed in the work of some of the more thoughtful writers on the current high levels of Western consumption such as Juliet Schor in the United States or Richard Eckersley and Clive Hamilton here in Australia. Whatever shortcomings mark the work of such writers, the key point that consumption matters and over-consumption matters a great deal must surely be listened to. These commentaries are also a million miles away from the timid politics of a culturalist reading of consumption that, by the late 1990s, had left itself with nothing else to say other than that consuming was a complex social activity. It is complex, and this is what is irritatingly overlooked within so many of the recent tomes on the evils of shopping. But then at least the new politics of consumption delivers a somewhat more confronting story.

The new critique of consumerism is in fact an indication of the 'after theory' return to politics identified by the British writer Terry Eagleton, among others. As Eagleton has recently observed, there is an unmistakable left/liberal return now to discussing fundamental questions of morality, nature, biology, religion and humanity both within and outside the academy, and doing so in a manner that does not fall back on a safe, complacent cultural constructionism or a depthless moral relativism. Importantly, this is evidenced not only within public intellectual discourses such as those over globalisation and overconsumption, but also within high theory itself, where there has been a vigorous and fruitful return to questions of the body, nature, time and the politics of change.

But the question here is about the exact nature of any such return to the political, and this is where the affluenza analysts go terribly wrong. All the talk of affluenza simply mirrors rather than reformulates a politics of consumption that saw its heyday in the 1950s and '60s with the publication of Vance Packard's *The Hidden Persuaders*, J.K. Galbraith's *The Affluent Society* and Herbert Marcuse's *One Dimensional Man*. These were formidable critiques, but for a different world, a different time. If the new anti-consumerism wants to present a newly calibrated critique, to present new possibilities, then it must break the mirror and reflect on its own ways of understanding the world it wants to challenge. This means imagining and utilising different and divergent ways of addressing consumerism, not simply recycling the old through an all-too-quick grab for easy pathological fictions.

Consumerism Has a Negative Impact on Society

Ron Scherer

In this selection, Ron Scherer describes the current economic condition America is facing: credit problems, outstanding loans, and a possible recession. He believes that American society is headed down a path of financial destruction, due to society moving away from meeting its basic needs, replacing this laudable goal with a spendthrift quest for materialistic ideals. Ron Scherer is a staff writer for the Christian Science Monitor.

Americans from Main Street to Wall Street may have to live with less debt.

Despite steeply lower short-term interest rates, banks and investors are now becoming much tougher when it comes to handing out credit cards, providing home-equity lines of credit, agreeing to lend money for corporate takeovers, and even providing money for student loans.

A Path of Economic Destruction

If this tougher scrutiny continues, economists see potential widespread ramifications for the economy:

- The tighter credit increases the possibility of a recession and makes any recovery less robust.

- If banks remain more selective in their lending, it could start to shift the roots of the economy from an emphasis on consumerism to savings.

Ron Scherer, "Credit Squeeze's Potential Ripple Effects," *Christian Science Monitor*, February 19, 2008. Copyright © 2008 The Christian Science Publishing Society. All rights reserved. Reproduced by permission from *Christian Science Monitor*, (www.csmonitor.com).

- It may become more difficult for Americans to buy houses for investment purposes, tempering any recovery in the housing market.

- Access to higher education could become more restricted. The credit markets have already made it harder for students with a bad credit history to borrow.

"We are wringing out the excesses from the frenzied times," says Mark Zandi, chief economist at Moody's Economy.com. "All this is happening very quickly."

The Effects of Consumerism in America

Last week [February 2008], Federal Reserve Chairman Ben Bernanke told Congress that the central bank's most recent survey of senior loan officers at large banks found further tightening of loan standards. "Credit that is more expensive and less available is a restraint on our economic growth," slated Mr. Bernanke in his testimony before the Senate Banking Committee.

At the heart of the changes are the enormous housing-loan losses that are coursing their way through bank earnings, insurance company portfolios, and even individual investors' accounts. As of the end of January, bank write-downs were about $120 billion, according to *The Wall Street Journal*. Analysts are now talking about $400 billion in total losses, about twice the estimates from last August when the problems in subprime mortgages became known.

"We still don't know who owns all those . . . products," says Dirk Nitzsche, a senior lecturer at the Case Business School in London. "It will probably take another six months to know where we stand and how much will have to be written off."

The uncertainty about the amount of bad debt is confounding even veterans of past credit crises. "I have been around a long time and been through all these credit situations in the last 50 years, and this is more opaque and more diverse and more global than any of these former difficulties," says Henry Kaufman, president of Henry Kaufman & Co. in New York. "At the moment it's too early to say if we have a structural change taking place or if this is a cyclical development."

Mr. Kaufman, a former chief economist at Salomon Brothers, says he does not doubt that banks will have to be less aggressive in lending unless they can significantly replenish their balance sheets.

"For marginal borrowers, it means it will be more difficult to get credit. And even those who are creditworthy, relatively speaking, are going to be paying more than under earlier circumstances," he says.

The potential effect of this credit squeeze, says Kaufman, is that even if there is no recession, "the economic recovery will be modest and moderate rather than dynamic." This slow growth period, he predicts, will "dampen" the financial markets for some time.

Economic Changes in Need for Consumers?

Mr. Zandi thinks the implications of the credit problems could be even larger. Since the 1980s, the consumer share of the gross domestic product (GDP) has been about 70 percent. "Over the next few decades, that will decline and go back to about 63 percent, which is where it was from World War II to the early 1980s."

Some signs are already emerging that some consumers are having trouble getting credit cards, says Bill Hardekopf, CEO of LowCards.com, a consumer resource center on credit cards. "We are seeing a tightening of approvals, and they are no longer granting approvals to people with marginal credit," he says.

The tightening is extending to home-equity lines of credit, says Richard DeKaser, chief economist at National City Corp.

in Cleveland. "The standard home-equity line used to be the prime interest rate [the interest rate charged to the best customers] minus half of a percentage point," he explains. "Now, we are starting to see prime minus one-quarter of a percentage point or just plain prime."

Individuals who have purchased their homes in the past year or two may even have negative equity in their homes since housing prices have fallen in many areas. "They would be unable to get the same line of credit," Mr. DeKaser says.

The reduction in home-equity lines could be particularly difficult for the economy because homeowners have tapped into them to modernize their homes, buy boats, or go on vacations. According to the Federal Reserve, as of Feb. 8 [2008] banks had $493.7 billion in outstanding lines of home-equity credit to individuals.

Lenders are also becoming much more selective in making loans to individuals who are buying homes for investment purposes. "One of the biggest elements of speculative borrowing was the Alt-A mortgage [a mortgage made to individuals who may not have a formal W-2 form, for example, meaning the borrower at least theoretically met the lender's requirements but didn't have all the documents," says DeKaser, "Buyers now will need more cash on their own. It's one of the reasons contributing to the decline in home sales in the last year."

Corporate Borrowers, Debt, and Credit

Corporate borrowers are likewise finding it harder to borrow and run up their debt. "We have not seen a real downturn in nonfinancial companies, but if that happens, the companies will have some problems in servicing their debt," says Mr. Kaufman. "It's one of the risks as we look into the second half of the year."

As investors become more cautious in their lending strategies, a greater load is falling on the banks, says DeKaser. This is showing up as a surge in commercial loans. "There is probably some crowding out going on, and lenders are becoming more choosy about where to extend credit," he says.

However, DeKaser warns against too much pessimism. "Just as we thought easy money would last forever, tight money won't last forever," he says. "I would caution against reading the moment as more permanent than it is."

The Rewards of Avoiding Consumerism

Lisa Leff

Lisa Leff is a writer for the Associated Press newswire service. In the following article, she describes a pledge taken by four friends to reduce their consumption for one year by buying nothing new save food and toiletries. Their pledge, which they called "The Compact," was emulated by other middle-class professionals in San Francisco and elsewhere. The four friends sought to increase their own awareness of the excesses of consumer culture and to make a difference to an economic system that they felt causes misery around the world. Rather than feeling deprived by their change in lifestyle, the group found the "shopping sabbatical" experience so liberating they decided to extend their boycott for another year.

It began, as grand ideas often do, over a dinner—risotto, artisan cheese and wine. What would it be like, 10 environmentally conscious friends wondered as they discussed the state of the planet, to go a year without buying anything new?

Twelve months later, the results from their experiment in anti-consumption for 2006 are in, and staying 100 percent true to the goal proved both harder and easier than those who signed on had expected.

And while broken vacuum cleaners and malfunctioning cellphones posed challenges, some of the group's original members said the self-imposed shopping sabbatical was so liberating that they have resolved to do it for another year.

"It started in a lighthearted way, but it is very serious," said John Perry, a father of two who works for a Silicon Valley

Lisa Leff, "Group Shuns Excessive Consumerism," *International Herald Tribune*, January 4, 2007. Copyright © 2007 The *International Herald Tribune*. Reprinted with permission.

technology company. "It is about being aware of the excesses of consumer culture and the fact we are drawing down our resources and making people miserable around the world."

The Compact

The pledge they half-jokingly named The Compact, after the Mayflower Pilgrims, spread to other cities through the Internet and an appearance on the "Today" show on NBC.

As it turned out, The Compact was modest as far as economic boycotts go. Several cities in the United States and Europe have communities of "freegans," people whose contempt for consumerism is so complete that they eat food foraged from Dumpsters whenever possible, train-hop and sleep in abandoned buildings on principle.

The San Francisco group, by contrast, exempted food, essential toiletries like toothpaste and shampoo, underwear and other purchases that fell under the categories of health and safety from their pledge. But perhaps because its members included middle-class professionals who could afford to shop recreationally, their cause caught on.

Nearly 3,000 people have joined a user group that Perry set up on Yahoo so participants could swap goods and tips.

Besides thrift stores and garage sales, participants found a wealth of free or previously owned merchandise in online classifieds and sites where people post stuff they want to get rid of, like www.freecycle.org.

Finding Out What You Really Need

After going through an initial period of retail withdrawal, discovering just how easy it was to score pretty much anything with a little time and effort was an eye-opener, according to participants.

Rachel Kesel, who works as a dog walker, said she was astonished by how often the items she needed simply materialized—the friend who offered a bicycle seat when hers was stolen, the Apple store employees who fixed her laptop at no cost.

Similarly fortuitous timing happened often enough that group members came up with a name for it—"Compact Karma."

After postponing purchases like a new jacket and a different stud for her pierced tongue—she could not bring herself to buy a used one—Kesel broke down only twice. Once was when she was planning a trip to Israel and could not find a used guidebook that reflected current political realities. The other was after her commuter coffee cup suffered a fatal crack. "I really found a lot of times there were things I thought I needed that I don't need that much," she said.

Changing One's Relationship with Things

The pledge provided unexpected dividends as well, like the joy of getting reacquainted with the local library and paying down credit cards. Gone, too, was the hangover of buyer's remorse.

Perry got satisfaction out of finding he had a knack for fixing things and how often manufacturers were willing to send replacement parts and manuals for products that had long since outlived their warranties. "One of the byproducts of The Compact has been I have a completely different relationship with the things in my life," he said. "I appreciate the stuff I have more." "I don't think I need to buy another pair of shoes until I'm entering Leisure World."

Over the holidays, Compact members gave homemade gifts or charitable donations in a recipient's name instead of engaging in the usual shopping crush.

Kate Boyd, a set designer and high school drama teacher, said she visited a new downtown shopping mall and felt like she had just stepped off a flying saucer.

"It was all stuff that had nothing to do with me, yet for so many people that's how they spend their weekends," she said. "It's entertainment, and it is the opposite of where I've been for a year."

Now that they know they can do it, Boyd, Kesel and Perry are ready to extend the pledge into 2007.

But first, they plan to give themselves a one-day reprieve to stock up on essentials, including windshield wipers, bicycle brakes and tongue studs.

Consumerism May Be the Religion of Our Time

Julian Baggini

Julian Baggini is a writer, philosopher, and editor and copublisher of the Philosophers' Magazine. *In the following article, he describes a scene at the opening of a branch in north London of the furniture chain store Ikea in which five people were hurt and twenty people suffered from heat exhaustion. Baggini compares the incident to religious pilgrimages in which people have also been trampled because of their fervor and desire to visit a particular shrine. For many people, he says, consumerism and the acquisition of material goods has supplanted the need for the spiritual; like religion, shopping promises, among other things, comfort and relief from suffering. He asks whether it would be a bad thing if consumerism has indeed become the new religion of our time.*

It's happened again. People have been "trampled by surging queues" leaving officials "deeply shocked, upset and concerned". One woman "pushed her way forward, screaming with excitement". There was a "crush" and a "scramble". "It was a stampede," according to one eyewitness; "You couldn't reason with these people, they were out of control." Stripped of the specifics of time and place, you would not know which recent event these quotes were describing. It could be [the] fracas [brawl] at Ikea in Edmonton, north London, in which five people were injured and around 20 suffered from heat exhaustion. Or maybe a similar incident at the Ikea in Jeddah [Saudi Arabia], in which three people lost their lives. Or it could be an account of how three died and 500 were injured in the "stoning of the devil" ritual near Mecca, during the hajj

Julian Baggini, "Assembly Required," The *Guardian*, February 12, 2005. © Guardian News and Media Limited 2007. Reproduced by permission.

[annual pilgrimage]. Or perhaps the much greater tragedy in which nearly 300 pilgrims died at the Mandher Devi temple during a Hindu pilgrimage near Wai in western India. In fact, the quotes are culled from reports of all four events. And without wishing to trivialise religion or the scale of the tragedy in Wai, the uncanny similarities between the reports of the pilgrims and the bargain hunters suggest that the idea that shopping is the new religion and Mammon our new God is one to be taken seriously.

Consider the Ikea incidents. It is characteristic of religions that they can motivate their followers to behave in ways that are inexplicable in terms of either rational self-interest or the welfare of the collective. It may be true that accidents at pilgrimages are usually triggered by the kinds of misfortunes that could happen anywhere, such as the wet steps and the electrical fire that contributed to the tragedy in Wai. But the causes have catastrophic effects only because people have put themselves in dangerously overcrowded situations. They do this not because it is good for them or others, but because they believe it is their religious duty. In the case of the Ikea crushes, the rational self-interest at work might be thought to be the large discounts being offered to shoppers. But a £45 leather sofa is not worth risking injury or even death for. The kind of "must have" mania that infects some shoppers as they close in on a good deal is more akin to the imperatives of religious devotion than those of personal finance. And the extent to which this can lead people to disregard the well-being of others caught up in the crush is astonishing.

Ikea Shoppers and Religious Pilgrims

Judged by their behaviour, the people who flock to Ikea during the sales really are like pilgrims flocking to a shrine or temple, while those who more calmly make their way to the shops at the weekend are akin to those who go to church on the sabbath. Shopping has taken on a whole raft of functions that religions used to take care of. Human beings seem to crave ritual, and shopping is the modern ritual par excellence. Many people will go shopping on the same day almost every week, visiting the same shops. They will stop off for a coffee at the usual time and will often meet friends while on their trips. The weekly shop provides comforting regularity, just as regular worship once did.

Religion also promises something higher, something transcendent to which we can aspire. You can ditch the metaphysics, but the same basic urge remains. So it is we now seek the higher in the material world, not the spiritual. The search for the comforts that will make our lives better and more meaningful now takes place in the pages of the Argos catalogue, not the Bible. That is why advertising is so often aspirational. Preachers seduce us with the promise of a better life to come, advertisers with the promise of a better life to come right now. Both offer an escape from the mundane reality and endless striving that real life is made of.

Of course, to point out similarities is not to establish an identity. What if consumerism had become a, if not the, religion of our time? Would that be an entirely bad thing? The religious and non-religious alike have cause to lament the replacement of what is either the true god or a false idol with something as empty as shopping. If the pioneers of the Enlightenment thought it would come to this, then they would not have been so optimistic about the prospects for human progress.

The Shift from the Spiritual to the Material

But there are reasons for being more sanguine about the shift from the spiritual to the material. People sometimes bemoan the relentless drift towards ever greater materialism as though history only ever moved in one direction. But there is little reason to suppose that we will get more and more materialistic as time goes by. Indeed, it's hard to see how we could.

What actually happens when people get relatively wealthy is that their minds often turn to other things. Bill Gates, for example, has given away astonishing amounts of money to help fight disease in the developing world, as well as devoting considerable time to his charitable work. Despite our apparent devotion to Mammon, we all know there are things money can't buy, which is why even those who want us to spend it, like Mastercard, acknowledge the fact.

Consumerism may not even be as bad for the poor as might be thought. Christianity has always had a strong social mission to alleviate the suffering of the poor. But it also sees a kind of virtue in poverty, not least in its ability to ease access to heaven. Consumerism may not care about the poor or address their needs directly, but it has no interest whatsoever in keeping them poor. It is far better for consumerism that they increase their wealth and spend it. Perhaps then the bargain-hunting pilgrims are not the vanguard of a new age of consumerist fundamentalism, but a manifestation of the post-religious world's immaturity. The change from a God- to a human-centred world view is, after all, very recent, and far from complete. It is not surprising that when we stopped looking to heaven for rewards and searched around us instead, the first things we lighted upon were material possessions. But it is precisely because, as those who oppose consumerism recognise, these things provide no lasting satisfaction, that as a society we are not doomed to become more and more in thrall to the retailers.

From this perspective, it may still be considered a shame that shopping is God and Ikea one of its most powerful churches. But at least we no longer comfort ourselves with illusions about the life beyond. At least our aspirations are for things that can be found in this life. And at least some of the things we buy really are worth having. The truth is, I rather like Ikea. I just don't worship it, that's all.

CHAPTER 2

The Impact
of Consumerism
on Humans

Consumerism Affects Health

John de Graaf, David Wann, and Thomas H. Naylor

John de Graaf is an author and frequent speaker on issues of overwork and overconsumption in America. David Wann is an author and video producer. Thomas H. Naylor is a writer, political activist, and professor emeritus of economics at Duke University. In the following chapter from their book Affluenza, *de Graaf, Wann, and Naylor show how consumerism affects Americans' health because it raises their levels of stress, which often manifests itself in physical illness and pain. The authors cite the findings of a medical doctor, Richard Swenson, who believes that his patients' physical complaints often have their roots in psychological disturbances that are the direct result of the frantic pace of life and possession overload that are the hallmarks of modern American life. They look at studies by economists and sociologists that confirm that overwork and lack of time has had devastating effects on people's mental and physical health.*

"Affluenza is a major disease, there's no question about it" says Dr. Richard Swenson of Menomonie, Wisconsin, who practiced medicine for many years before changing his focus to writing and lecturing. A tall, bearded, deeply religious man, Swenson began over a period of time to conclude that much of the pain in his patients' lives had psychological rather than physical roots. "And after about four or five years, the whole idea of *margin* came to the surface," he says. He found that too many of his patients were stretched to their limits and beyond with no margin, no room in their lives for rest, relaxation, and reflection. They showed symptoms of acute stress.

"It could be physical symptoms," Swenson recalls. "Headaches, low back pain, hyperacidity, palpitations in the heart, unexplained aches and pains. Or it could be emotional problems like depression, anxiety, sleeplessness, irritability, yelling at your boss or at your colleagues or your kids. There were all kinds of behavioral symptoms like driving too fast or drinking too much or screaming too much or being abusive. I recognized that they didn't have any space in their lives, they didn't have any reserves. The space between their load and their limits had just disappeared. I couldn't take an X-ray to find this thing, but nevertheless it was there. And it was a powerful source of pain and dysfunction in people's lives."

Possession Overload

Swenson observed that many of his patients suffered from what he now calls "possession overload," the problem of dealing with too much stuff. "Possession overload is the kind of problem where you have so many things you find your life is being taken up by maintaining and caring for things instead of people," Swenson says. "Everything I own owns me. People feel sad and what do they do? They go to the mall and they shop and it makes them feel better, but only for a short time. There's an addictive quality in consumerism. But it simply doesn't work. They've gotten all these things and they still find this emptiness, this hollowness. All they have is stress and exhaustion and burnout, and their relationships are vaporizing. They're surrounded by all kinds of fun toys but the meaning is gone."

"Tragedy," observes Swenson, "is wanting something badly, getting it, and finding it empty. And I think that's what's happened."

Time Famine

There's been an almost imperceptible change in American greetings over the past two decades. Remember how when you used to say "how are you?" to the friends you ran into at work or on the street, they'd reply "fine, and you?" Now, when we ask that question, the answer is often "busy, and you?" (when they have time to say, "and you?") "Me too," we admit. We used to talk of having "time to smell the flowers." Now we barely find time to smell the coffee. "The pace of life has accelerated to the point where everyone is breathless," says Richard Swenson. "You look at all the countries that have the most prosperity and they're the same countries that have the most stress."

Tried to make a dinner date with a friend recently? Chances are you have to look a month ahead in your appointment calendars. Even children now carry them. Ask your co-workers what they'd like more of in their lives and odds are they'll say "time." "This is an issue that cuts across race lines, class lines, and gender lines," says African-American novelist Barbara Neely. "Nobody has any time out there." We're all like the bespectacled bunny in Disney's *Alice in Wonderland*, who keeps looking at his watch and muttering, "No time to say hello, goodbye, I'm late! I'm late! I'm late!"

By the early 1990s, trend-spotters were warning that a specter was haunting America: time famine. Advertisers noted that "time will be the luxury of the 1990s." A series of clever TV spots for US West showed time-pressed citizens trying to "buy time" at a bank called 'Time R Us' or in bargain basements. One store offered customers "the greatest sale of all TIME." A weary woman asked where she could buy "quality time." "Now you CAN buy time," the ads promised. "Extra working time with mobile phone service from US West."

More working time. Hmmm.

We thought the opposite was supposed to be true: that advances in technology, automation, cybernation, were supposed to give us more leisure time and *less* working time. Remember how all those futurists were predicting that by the end of the 20th Century we'd have more leisure time than we'd know what to do with? In 1965, a U.S. Senate subcommittee heard testimony that estimated a workweek of from fourteen to twenty-two hours by the year 2000.

We got the technology, but we didn't get the time. We have computers, fax machines, cell phones, e-mail, robots, express mail, freeways, jetliners, microwaves, fast food, one-hour photos, digital cameras, pop tarts, frozen waffles, instant this and instant that. But we have *less* free time than we did thirty years ago. And about those mobile phones: They do give you "extra working time" while driving, but make you as likely to cause an accident as someone who's legally drunk. Progress? And then there are those leaf blowers. . . .

Patience may be the ultimate victim of our hurried lives. David Schenk, the author of *The End of Patience*, says that such things as the speed of the Internet for e-mail and on-line shopping mean that "we're packing more into our lives and losing patience in the process. We've managed to compress time to such an extent that we're now painfully aware of every second that we wait for anything." There are now Internet news monitors in the elevators of a large Northeast hotel chain, and the ability to pedal and surf the Net at the same time at many fitness centers. Gas stations are considering putting in TV monitors on the islands to keep you amused while pumping.

The Harried Leisure Class

We should have paid attention to Staffan Linder. In 1970, the Swedish economist warned that all those predictions about more free time were a myth, that we'd soon be a "harried leisure class" starved for time. "Economic growth," wrote Linder, "entails a general increase in the scarcity of time." He continued, "As the volume of consumption goods increases, requirements for the care and maintenance of these goods also tends to increase, we get bigger houses to clean, a car to wash, a boat to put up for the winter, a television set to repair, and have to make more decisions on spending."

It's as simple as this: increased susceptibility to affluenza means increasing headaches from time pressure.

Shopping itself, Linder pointed out "is a very time-consuming activity." Indeed, on average, Americans now spend nearly seven times as much time shopping as they do playing with their kids. Even our celebrated freedom of choice only adds to the problem.

Brand A or Brand B?

Consider the average supermarket. It now contains 30,000 items, two and a half times as many as it did twenty years ago. Picture yourself having to choose between a hundred types of cereal, for instance (or almost any other item). You can decide by price, grabbing what's on sale; by flavor—sweet sells—or by nutrition—but then, what counts most? Protein? Cholesterol? Calories? Added vitamins? Fat? Dietary fiber? Or you can give in to your child's nagging and buy the Cocoa Puffs. You can reach for tomato juice, confident that you're getting vitamins and antioxidants and only fifty calories per serving. But don't look at the "sodium" column—you won't be able to allow yourself any more salt for the rest of the day without feeling guilty.

Psychologist Barry Schwartz, in his book *The Paradox of Choice*, warns that having so many choices increases our anxiety and is likely to leave us less happy. He points out that many of us are regularly troubled by the sense that we may have made the wrong choice, that we could have gotten a better product or a lower price.

So many choices. So little time. Linder said this would happen, and he warned that when choices become overwhelming, "the emphasis in advertising will be placed on ersatz information," because "brand loyalty must be built up among people who have no possibility of deciding how to act on objective grounds." Ergo, if you're a marketer, hire a battery of psychologists to study which box colors are most associated by shoppers with pleasurable sex. Or something else you might want.

Overworking Americans

Linder argued that past a certain point, time pressure would increase with growing productivity. But he wasn't sure whether working hours would rise or fall. He certainly doubted they'd fall as much as the automation cheerleaders predicted. He was right. In fact, there seems to be some pretty strong evidence that Americans are actually working more now than they did a generation ago.

Using U.S. Department of Labor statistics, Boston College sociologist Juliet Schor argues that full-time American workers are now toiling 160 hours—one full month—*more*, on average, than they did in 1969. "It's not only the people in the higher income groups—who, by the way, have been working much longer hours," says Schor. "It's also the middle classes, the lower classes, and the poor. Everybody is working longer hours." Indeed, according to the International Labor Organization, in October of 1999 the United States passed Japan as the modern industrial country with the longest working hours. Forty-two percent of American workers say they feel "used up" by the end of the workday. Sixty-nine percent say they'd like to slow down and live a more relaxed life.

No Time to Care

Moreover, Schor says, "The pace of work has increased quite dramatically. We are working much faster today than we were in the past. And that contributes to our sense of being overworked and frenzied and harried and stressed out and burned out by our jobs." In the fax lane, everybody wants that report yesterday. Patience wears thin rapidly when we get used to a new generation of computers.

Several years ago, Karen Nussbaum, former president of 9 to 5, a clerical workers union, pointed out that "twenty-six million Americans are monitored by the machines they work on, and that number is growing. I had one woman tell me her computer would flash off and on: YOU'RE NOT WORKING AS FAST AS THE PERSON NEXT TO YOU!" Doesn't just thinking about that make your blood pressure rise?

Sometimes the speedup reaches utterly inhumane levels. In late May 2000, evening newscasts across the Northwest showed disturbing footage taken inside the Iowa Beef Processors slaughterhouse in Wallula, Washington. The video showed cattle being struck on the head, electrically prodded, and hoisted in the air as they moved down the slaughtering line, kicking and struggling. Fully conscious cows were skinned alive and had their legs cut off. In a signed affidavit, one employee said, "The chain goes too fast, more than 300 cows an hour. If I can't get the animal knocked out right, it keeps going. It never stops. The cows are getting hung alive or not alive. I can tell some cows are alive because they're holding their heads up. They just keep coming, coming, coming. . . ." The video provides gruesome evidence that the speed of American production, driven by an insatiable desire for more, virtually guarantees us no time to care.

Choosing Stuff over Time

Meanwhile, we have less time to recuperate from the work frenzy. A survey by Expedia.com found that Americans gave back an average of three vacation days to their employees in 2003, a gift to corporations of $20 billion. As their reason for doing so, most said they didn't want to be seen as slackers when the next round of layoffs came. Others said they simply couldn't take time off and keep up with the demands of their jobs.

Juliet Schor reminds us that the United States has seen more than a doubling of productivity since World War II. "So the issue is: what do we do with that progress? We could cut back on working hours. We could produce the old amount in half as much time and take half the time off. Or we could work just as much and produce twice as much?" And, says Schor, "we've put all our economic progress into producing more things. Our consumption has doubled and working hours have not fallen at all. In fact, working hours have risen."

Europeans made a different decision. In 1970, worker productivity per hour in the countries that make up the European Union [EU] was 65 percent that of Americans. Their GDP [gross domestic product] per capita was about 70 percent of ours because they worked longer than we did back then. Today, EU productivity stands at 91 percent of ours, and several European economies are more productive per worker hour than we are. But real per capita GDP in those countries is still only about 72 percent that of the United States. They have a lot less stuff than we do. So what happened? It's simple: the Europeans traded a good part of their productivity gains for time instead of money. So instead of working more than we do, they now work much less—nearly nine weeks less per year.

As a result, they live longer and are healthier, despite spending far, far less per capita on health care. In fact, the United States ranks dead last in health among industrial nations, and we are now expected to spend 19 percent of our total GDP on health care by the year 2014. Can you say "Mister Yuck?"

Not everyone agrees with Schor about longer working hours. John Robinson, who runs the Americans' Use of Time Project at the University of Maryland, claims that "time diaries" kept by employees (they record how they spend each minute of every workday) actually show a decrease in working hours. But Robinson does agree that most working Americans "feel" more time-pressured than ever. Much of their increased leisure, he says, has been consumed in watching television—and thus by absorbing even more exhortations to consume.

He also agrees that Europeans work far less and spend much more time socializing—which has proved to be good for health.

Whether one accepts Schor's numbers or Robinson's, the experience of time famine intensifies, driven by longer, or at least more demanding, working hours, and the competing time requirements associated with the care and feeding of stuff. Something has got to give. For many Americans, it's sleep. Many doctors say more than half of all Americans get too little sleep—an average of an hour too little each night. We average 20 percent less sleep than we did in 1900. And that takes a toll on health (not to mention the 100,000 traffic accidents each year that result from drivers falling asleep at the wheel). So does our urgency about time.

Heart Attacks Waiting to Happen

The intake examination at the Meyer Friedman Institute in San Francisco is like none other in a doctor's office. A nurse runs prospective patients through a series of questions about their relationship to time. "Do you walk fast? Do you eat fast? Do you often do two or more things at the same time?" She also notes their physical responses to her questions. "Something you do a lot," she tells one interviewee, "is what we call expiratory sighing, as if you're emotionally exhausted or don't even want to think about the matter I'm asking you to talk about."

The nurse tabulates the answers provided by patients and gives them a score, putting most squarely in the category that, years ago, the late Meyer Friedman called the Type A personality. While working on the *Affluenza* film, John took the test and asked the nurse how he did. "You're right in the middle," she said, smiling. "You mean, like A minus, B plus?" John quizzed her. "I'm afraid not," she replied. "You're right in the middle of Type A. However, if it's any consolation, you're less Type A than most people in your profession." Unconsoled,

John is working on slowing down (is that an oxymoron?). For the first time ever, he's trying to *lower* his grade.

The more Type A someone is, the more likely that person is to suffer from what Dr. Friedman called "time urgency." "We've also called it hurry sickness in the past," Bart Sparagon, the mellow, soft-spoken doctor who now directs Friedman's clinic, says slowly. "It's as if people are struggling against time."

"I have a vivid image of an advertisement for a famous journal about financial affairs," Sparagon adds, with a look of resignation. "It's a picture of men in suits carrying briefcases, leaping over hurdles, with this hostile, tense look on their faces, and it's an ad suggesting that if you buy this magazine, you can win this race. But when I see that picture, I know those men are racing toward a heart attack. I mean, do you *want* to win that race?"

Along with time urgency, the racers usually are afflicted with what Meyer Friedman terms "free-floating hostility." Everything that causes them to slow down—in their pursuit of money or other symbols of success—becomes an enemy, something in their way, an obstacle to overcome. "I think that time urgency is the major cause of premature heart disease in this country," Meyer Friedman once declared. The more Type A a person is, he believes, the greater that person's risk of cardiac arrest.

Affluenza is certainly not the only cause of time urgency. But it is a major cause. Swelling expectations lead to a constant effort to keep up with the latest products, to compete in the consumption arena. That, in turn, forces us to work more, so we can afford the stuff. With so many things to use, and the need to work harder to obtain them, our lives grow more harried and pressured. As one pundit put it, "If you win the rat race, you're still a rat." And you may be a dead one.

In recent years, many scientists have come to believe that viruses and other infections make us more susceptible to heart attacks. Their conclusions have come from studying influenza viruses. But if Meyer Friedman and his theories about Type A personalities are right, they should look more closely at affluenza as well.

Consumer Capitalism Induces Childishness

Benjamin R. Barber

Benjamin R. Barber is the Kekst Professor of Civil Society at the University of Maryland and a Distinguished Fellow at Demos in New York City. He consults with political and civil leaders throughout the world on democratization, culture, and education. In the following article, he describes how consumer culture in the United States has created a society of perennial adolescents. This induced childishness, he argues, is needed to drive the global market economy as it now exists, but also threatens to undermine capitalism itself. Barber asks whether markets can be made to meet the real needs capitalism is designed to serve.

In these paltry times of capitalism's triumph, as we slide into consumer narcissism, Shakespeare's seven ages of man are in danger of being washed away by lifelong puerility [childishness]. Pop-cultural journalists have used many terms to depict a new species of perennial adolescent: *kidults, rejuveniles, twixters*, and *adultescents*; around the world Germans speak of "Nesthocker," Italians of "Mammone," Japanese of "Freeter," Indians of "Zippies," and the French of a "Tanguy" syndrome and "puériculture." What they are discerning with their pop neologisms is the consequence of a powerful new cultural ethos, felt more than recognized. It is an ethos of induced childishness: an infantilization that is closely tied to the demands of consumer capitalism in a global market economy.

This infantilist ethos is as potent in shaping the ideology and behaviors of our radical consumerist society today as what [German social scientist] Max Weber called the "Protestant ethic" was in shaping the entrepreneurial culture of what was then a productivist early capitalist society. Affiliated with an ideology of privatization, the marketing of brands, and a homogenization of taste, this ethos of infantilization has worked to sustain consumer capitalism, but at the expense of both civility and civilization and at a growing risk to capitalism itself. Although we use the term *democratic capitalism* in a manner that suggests a certain redundancy, the reality is that the two words describe different systems often in tension with one another. Consumerism has set the two entirely asunder.

How much should we care? In an epoch when terrorism stalks the planet, when fear of Jihad [Islamic holy war] is as prevalent as the infringement of liberties to which fear gives rise, when AIDS and tsunamis and war and genocide put democracy at risk in both the developing and the developed world, it may seem self-indulgent to fret about the dangers of hyperconsumerism. When poor children in the developing world are being exploited, starved, prostituted, and impressed into military service, anxiety about the prosperous young in the developed world who may be growing up into consumers too fast, or about adult consumers being dumbed down too easily, can seem parochial, even solipsistic [self-indulgent].

The Pathologies of Liberty

Yet as James Madison said long ago, the pathologies of liberty can be as perilous as the pathologies of tyranny; and far more difficult to discern or remedy. Although forces of Jihad continue to struggle violently against the successes of McWorld, and the abuse of children living under poverty remains a far greater problem than the infantilization of adults living under prosperity, modernization appears to be irreversible over the long term. But the fate of citizens under capitalism triumphant is another matter. The victory of consumers is not synonymous with the victory of citizens. McWorld can prevail and liberty can still lose. The diseases of prosperity which are the afflictions of capitalism do not kill outright. They violate no explicit laws of justice. Yet capitalism's success breeds new and dangerous challenges.

Capitalism per se is not the issue. The question is not whether there is an alternative to markets but whether markets can be made to meet the real needs capitalism is designed to serve, whether capitalism can adapt to the sovereignty of democratic authority that alone will allow it to survive.

Once upon a time, capitalism was allied with virtues that also contributed at least marginally to democracy, responsibility and citizenship. Today it is allied with vices which—although they serve consumerism—undermine democracy, responsibility, and citizenship. The question then is whether not just democracy but capitalism itself can survive the infantilist ethos upon which it has come to depend. . . . What is clear is that either capitalism will replace the infantilist ethos with a democratic ethos, and regain its capacity to promote equality as well as profit, diversity as well as consumption, or infantilization will undo not only democracy but capitalism itself. Much will depend on our capacity to make sense out of infantilization and relate it to the not-so-creative destruction of consumerism's survival logic.

The Infantilization of America

The idea of an "infantilist ethos" is as provocative and controversial as the idea of what Weber called the "Protestant ethic." *Infantilization* is at once both an elusive *and* a confrontational term, a potent metaphor that points on the one hand to the dumbing down of goods and shoppers in a postmodern global economy that seems to produce more goods than people need; and that points, on the other hand, to the targeting of children as consumers in a market where there are never enough shoppers. Once a staple of Freudian psychology focused on the psychopathology of regression, the term *infantilization* has in the last several years become a favorite of worrywart journalists: David Ansen fretting about the "widespread infantilization of pop culture"; Leon Wieseltier charging that "Hollywood is significantly responsible for the infantilization of America;" Philip Hensher of Britain's *The Independent* sure that the "signs that adult culture is being infantilized are everywhere."

On the potency of adolescent culture, liberals and conservatives agree. Writes Robert J. Samuelson, a moderate liberal: "We live in an age when people increasingly refuse to act their age. The young (or many of them) yearn to be older, while the older (or many of them) yearn to be younger. We have progressively demolished the life cycle's traditional stages, shortening childhood and following it with a few murky passages. Adolescence . . . begins before puberty and, for some, lasts forever . . . age denial is everywhere." Samuelson is echoed by Joseph Epstein, a moderate conservative: "The whole sweep of advertising, which is to say of market, culture since soon after World War II has been continuously to lower the criteria of youthfulness while extending the possibility for seeming youthful to older and older people." Even conservatives who reject the charge of consumer infantilization recognize its potency. George F. Will thus charges progressive thinkers with advancing the thesis of the "infantilism of the American public" as one more "we are all victims of manipulation" explanation for Bush's victory in the 2004 presidential campaign. Little surprise then that popular magazines such as *Time* ("They Just Won't Grow Up") and *New York Magazine* ("Forever Youngish: Why Nobody Wants to Be an Adult Anymore") worry in major cover articles about America's Peter Pan tendencies.

There is anecdotal evidence everywhere: airport police handing out lollipops to placate irate passengers at inspection points; television news divisions turned over to entertainment executives, *Vanity Fair*–style pop-cultural chatter about "enfantrepreneurs," and the *New York Times Magazine* enthusing about "what kids want in fashion, right from the filly's mouth" on the way to urging thongs on seven-year-olds; the professionalization of high-school sports that turns teen basketball courts into NBA recruiting turf and basketball-player bodies into advertising billboards; adult fiction readers flocking to *Harry Potter* and *The Lord of the Rings* (when they are not abandoning reading altogether); fast-food franchises girdling the world to exploit (among other things) children's restless aversion to grown-up sit-down dining; teen guy games such as World of Warcraft, Grand Theft Auto, and Narc and comic-book films such as *Terminator, Spider-Man, Catwoman*, and *Shrek* dominating the entertainment market; new "educational" television channels such as BabyFirstTV and videos such as "Baby Einstein"; cosmetic surgery and Botox injections promising a fountain of youth to female baby boomers who envy their daughters; sexual performance drugs such as Levitra, Cialis, and Viagra (2002 sales of over $1 billion) becoming staples of equally uncomfortable male boomers trying to smuggle atavistic youth into the age of social security; and businessmen in baseball caps, jeans, and untucked shirts mimicking the studied sloppiness of their unformed kids. Beyond pop culture, the infantilist ethos also dominates: dogmatic judgments of black and white in politics and religion come to displace the nuanced complexities of adult morality, while the marks of perpetual childishness are grafted onto adults who indulge in puerility without pleasure, and indolence without innocence. Hence, the new consumer penchant for age without dignity, dress without formality, sex without reproduction, work without discipline, play without spontaneity, acquisition without purpose, certainty without doubt, life without responsibility, and narcissism into old age and unto death without a hint of wisdom or humility. In the epoch in which we now live, civilization is not an ideal or an aspiration, it is a video game.

Creating an Adolescent Cultural Ethos

These myriad anecdotes tell a story, but infantilization—not second childhood but enduring childishness—is much more than just a mesmeric [hypnotic] metaphor. A new cultural ethos is being forged that is intimately associated with global consumerism. Those responsible for manufacturing and merchandizing goods for the global marketplace, those who are actually researching, teaching, and practicing marketing and advertising today, are aiming both to sell to a younger demographic and to imbue older consumers with the tastes of the young.

Marketers and merchandisers are self-consciously chasing a youthful commercial constituency sufficiently padded in its pocketbook to be a very attractive market, yet sufficiently unformed in its tastes as to be vulnerable to conscious corporate manipulation via advertising, marketing, and branding. At the same time, these avatars of consumer capitalism are seeking to encourage adult regression, hoping to rekindle in grown-ups the tastes and habits of children so that they can sell globally the relatively useless cornucopia of games, gadgets, and myriad consumer goods for which there is no discernible "need market" other than the one created by capitalism's own frantic imperative to sell. As child-development scholar Susan Linn puts it in her critical study of what she calls "the hostile takeover of childhood," corporations are vying "more and more aggressively for young consumers" while popular culture "is being smothered by commercial culture relentlessly sold to children who [are valued] for their consumption."

As the population in the developed world ages—the irony of infantilization—the definition of youth simply moves up, with baby boomers in the United States smuggling it into their senior years. Meanwhile, the young are big spenders way before they are even modest earners: in 2000, there were 31 million American kids between twelve and nineteen already controlling 155 billion consumer dollars. Just four years later, there were 33.5 million kids controlling $169 billion, or roughly $91 per week per kid. The potential youth market is even more impressive elsewhere in the world, where a far greater proportion of the population is under twenty-five, and where new prosperity in nations such as India and China promises a youth market of hundreds of millions in the coming years.

The Economist summed it up a few years ago in its millennium special report: "Once, when you grew up you put away childish things. Today, the 35-year-old Wall Street analyst who zips to work on his push-scooter, listening to Moby on his headphones and carrying annual reports in his backpack, has far more in common with a 20-year-old than he would have done a generation ago." John Tierney notes in the *New York Times* that Americans are marrying older (since 1970 the median age for marriage has moved up four years, to twenty-five for women and twenty-seven for men), and that thirty is the new twenty, and forty is the new thirty. In Hollywood, where aspiring to stay young is as old as movies and everything is hyperbole, "40 is the new 30 and 50 the new 40, but only, it seems, when that new 40 and 50 have been surgically enhanced. . . . These days, when a 40-plus-year-old actress lands a starring part opposite a 60-plus-year-old actor, such age-appropriate casting seems meaningless because the actress has a face as unlined as a teenage girl's."

As many as four million not-so-young adults between twenty-five and thirty-four still live with their parents in the United States, many of them middle-class. In Britain, the Office for National Statistics revealed the same trend, noting that "57 per cent of men and 38 per cent of women aged 20–24 are now living with their parents." According to the 2005 report, "by their late 20s more than one in five men still live at their parents' homes, twice the rate of women." "Unencumbered by rent—or mortgages or children," these stay-at-homes have "lots of disposable income, which is why marketers have happily focused on adultescents since at least 1996." A physicians' organization called the Society for Adolescent Medicine reports on its website that it is concerned with people ten to twenty-six years old, while the MacArthur Foundation's "Transitions to Adulthood" project puts the transition's end at thirty-four years old.

Growing Chronologically Older but Younger in Behavior

The irony of infantilization is, of course, that Americans are actually getting older, the median age having moved from twenty-five in the baby-boomer high-water year of 1960 to thirty-five in 2000; by 2050 there will be more in their seventies than in their teens. The same is true with a vengeance for Europe, and for the indigenous populations (immigrants excluded) of the developed world generally. Only in the Third World and in the Third World immigrant communities of the First World is the majority constituted by the young—although they often lack the means to express their puerility in consumption. Likewise, in the United States, more than a third of those who live below the poverty line are children, who like their cousins in the developing world are relatively insulated by their poverty from the consequences, if not the temptations, of consumer marketing.

Once upon a time, in capitalism's more creative and successful period, a *productivist* capitalism prospered by meeting the real needs of real people. Creating a synergy between making money and helping others (the Puritan Protestant formula for entrepreneurial virtue), producers profited by making commodities for the workers they employed—a circle of virtue that, while it involved elements of risk-taking for producers and exploitation of workers, benefited both classes and society at large. Today, however, consumerist capitalism profits only when it can address those whose essential needs have already been satisfied but who have the means to assuage "new" and invented needs—[Karl] Marx's "imaginary needs." The global majority still has extensive and real natural needs mirroring what psychologists T. Berry Brazelton and Stanley I. Greenspan have called "the irreducible needs of children." But it is without the means to address them, being cut off by the global market's inequality (the "north/south divide") from the investment in capital and jobs that would allow them to become consumers. This is true not just for the global Third World but for the growing Third World within the First World, the poor who live among the wealthy, exposed to the seductions of the consumer marketplace but without the means to participate in it.

Denizens of the developed world from North America and Europe to Korea and Japan grow older chronologically but younger in their behavior, style, and controlling ethos, with children dominating consumer markets and the taste cultures that support them in ways that subvert adult culture. Elsewhere in the developing world, though the demographic grows younger (recall the familiar fact that more than half of the population of the Middle East is under sixteen), children remain marginalized and in poverty, irrelevant as consumers despite their overwhelming needs and forced to grow up prematurely, becoming little soldiers, little prostitutes, and little garment-factory workers, giving some to the global market economy but gaining little from it. They are wholly disempowered even where they are used and abused. And they are always the first to pay the cost of global economic inequalities. Their needs are ignored by global capitalism since they have no disposable income to pay for them. Even the World Bank and the International Monetary Fund, the institutions charged with responding to their needs, impose "conditionality" on the aid and loans with which they purport to alleviate their problems. "Corrupt" and "inefficient" Third World governments are punished; the kids starve, fall ill, and die. In war and poverty, in natural disaster and man-made genocide, they are most often the first victims and the last to benefit from capitalism's otherwise voracious appetite for consumers.

In this new epoch in which the needy are without income and the well-heeled are without needs, radical inequality is simply assumed. The United States and Canada, for example, with just over 5 percent of the world's population, control almost one-third (31.5 percent) of the world's private consumption expenditures. Western Europe, with 6.4 percent of the population, controls almost 29 percent of expenditures—that means 11.5 percent of the world's population controls 60 percent of the world's consumer spending. On the other hand, sub-Saharan Africa, with nearly 11 percent of the population, controls only 1.2 percent of consumer expenditures.

Raising New Generations of Consumers

Inequality leaves capitalism with a dilemma: the overproducing capitalist market must either grow or expire. If the poor cannot be enriched enough to become consumers, then grown-ups in the First World who are currently responsible for 60 percent of the world's consumption, and with vast disposable income but few needs, will have to be enticed into shopping. Inducing them to remain childish and impetuous in their taste helps ensure that they will buy the global market goods designed for indolent and prosperous youth. When translated into figures for comparative spending on advertising versus spending on foreign aid, these grim inequalities yield a remarkable contrast: while the United States spent about $16 billion in foreign aid in 2003, the projected American expenditure for advertising for 2005 was $276 billion (about one-half of the world's projected advertising expenditure for 2005). If manufacturing needs rather than goods is a primary task of consumer capitalism, however, the massive advertising and marketing budgets are understandable.

Marx himself had remarked in the *Communist Manifesto* of 1848 on the dislodging of old-fashioned industries by new industries in which "in place of old wants, we find new wants." Calvin Coolidge had presciently depicted advertising as "the method by which the desire is created for better things," anticipating by nearly forty years Guy Debord's more radical claim in the 1960s that "the satisfaction of primary human needs, [is] now met in the most summary manner, by a ceaseless manufacture of pseudoneeds." Many of the needs of children that can be regarded as "irreducible," on the other hand, cannot be met by the market at all, but depend on kinship relations, parenting, self-image, learning, and limit-setting. Because so many needs are beyond what capitalism produces and sells, capitalism demands what [economist John Maynard] Keynes called a certain "pumping up" of purchasing power. The founder of Filene's department store, on a visit to Paris back in 1935, grasped even then that (in [historian] Victoria de Grazia's description) "the chief economic problem facing the industrial world was to distribute goods in accordance with the now patently inexhaustible capacity to produce them. Not the overproduction of merchandise, but its nondistribution was the problem." From the point of view of business-people, they were not producing too much, consumers were buying too little.

This was a theme that coursed through consumerist capitalism from the start. By our own times, it was a theme picked up by marketers for whom the fabricating of needs seemed the better part of wisdom. We no longer have to reference [author] Vance Packard's warning about hidden persuaders: the persuaders have come out of the closet and are teaching corporate managers the arts of marketing to teens at national conferences and are articulating toddler marketing techniques in textbooks and business-school marketing courses. Nor do we need [French social scientist] Herbert Marcuse's subtle argument about the one-dimensionality of modern men: clever marketing consultants are openly subverting pluralistic human identity in pursuit not simply of brand loyalty but of lifelong brand identity.

In other words, I am not reading the notion of infantilization into what the market is doing in order to illuminate its practices in an era of mandatory selling; I am extrapolating out of the actual practices of the consumer marketplace the idea of pumping up purchasing power, manufacturing needs, and encouraging infantilization. I am not suggesting in the passive voice that there "is a process of infantilization under way." I am arguing that many of our primary business, educational, and governmental institutions are consciously and purposefully engaged in infantilization and as a consequence that we are vulnerable to such associated practices as privatization and branding. For this is how we maintain a system of consumerist capitalism no longer supported by the traditional market forces of supply and demand.

Advertising Links Identity with Consumerism

Dinyar Godrej

Dinyar Godrej is coeditor of the New Internationalist *magazine. In the following article, he describes how advertising manipulates consumers by tapping into the subconscious mind. Because of advertisers' tactics, it is not as easy as one would think to make an informed and conscious choice about how to spend one's money. Further, he explains, the information available to American audiences from the news media is largely driven by advertising—what is shown on the news is directly related to the advertising dollars that sponsor it—which further skews their perspective. Advertising, says Godrej, while necessary to an extent, has gotten out of hand—the worldview it promotes is out of touch with real life. Corporate giants sugar-coat their names by making conspicuous charitable donations and doing good, promoting images of themselves in their ads that are misleading simply to increase their profits. However, he says, there is hope, and independent media can help consumers recognize the truth behind corporate ads and to resist irrational urges to buy.*

Buddhism and Hinduism recommend it. A retreat from clamour, a wondrous detachment that allows the material world to float up, like a sloughed-off skin, for one's dispassionate consideration. Whether they offer useful advice on re-engaging after this revelation, I don't know. The first astronauts saw a floating world, too. It provoked suitably joined-up thoughts about its (and our) fragility and essential unity.

But there are other worlds. And the one that elbows itself to the front of our attention's queue painstakingly creates surface and whips up froth. It's the one that the 125 residents of

Dinyar Godrej, "The Ad Industry Pins Us Down," *New Internationalist*, September 2005. Reproduced by permission.

Clark, Texas, signed up to in 2005 when they changed the name of their township to Dish in return for a decade's free cable TV from the DISH Network. Hey, what's in a name except a wacky corporate PR opportunity, right?

The bubbly, dazzling world of which Dish has become an emblem shows little sign of floating up for our inspection. If we inspect it nonetheless, it reveals itself to be firmly riveted down by that old culprit—disproportionate corporate power.

Advertising is a bit of a compulsive liar. In the early days it was quite bare-faced—the beverage giant, Dewar's, claiming in the 1930s that their Scotch whiskey repelled colds and flu; cigarette brands claiming that they soothed the throat and helped asthma. Some of this still goes on. Quack cures are advertised in numerous Majority World countries. The half of all Mexican citizens who are overweight are pummelled daily on TV by products that promise to melt 10 centimetres off the waistline in two hours.

Repeat After Me

Nowadays, regulatory bodies will see off many of the more obviously fraudulent claims.

But advertising is involved in soul fraud instead. If that sounds a bit deep, just stay with me a while.

Advertising today has little to do with introducing a new product or describing an existing one's virtues. It has everything to do with images, dreams and emotions; stuff we are evolutionarily programmed to engage with but which is, almost without exception in the ad biz, fake. Imagine how much attention you would pay if there were just text and no images. When ads for Sprite (owned by Coca-Cola) proclaimed: 'Image is nothing, thirst is everything', they were reassuring people that they were right to be distrustful, while building up images of honesty and straight talk, using professional basketball players to push the product. Sprite jumped several notches up the soft-drink rankings; moolah was minted. Image was everything, even if it was purporting to be an anti-image. Amid the visual clutter, advertising—the chief agent of the mess—has to jump out at us. It must trigger off associations, however tangential, that will keep our attention. Endless repetition through media channels should build up a handy cloud of associations. According to one industry executive: 'In the context of most advertising, particularly passively consumed media like television and cinema, learning is incidental, not deliberate. This is why people tell you they are not influenced by advertising. They are not actively trying to take anything away from the experience, and therefore are not influenced at that time; but the effects will show up later, long after a particular viewing experience is forgotten.'

Much effort is expended upon trying to sink boreholes into the vast iceberg of the subconscious mind, probably because the products being flogged are in reality just variations on the same old same old. A recent buzzword is 'neuromarketing'. Neuroscientists and psychiatrists are searching for the buy-button in the brain. This involves putting subjects into brain-scanning machinery and pitching concepts and images at them to see which ones make the lights flash. In one experiment, subjects were made to blind-taste Pepsi and Coke. Pepsi scored higher in terms of response in the ventral putamen, the part of the brain associated with feelings of reward—ie, most thought Pepsi tasted better. But when the subjects were informed which drink was Coke before they tried it, their medial prefrontal cortexes lit up. This is an area of the brain believed to control cognition. Most now said they preferred Coke. So just the name had prompted memories and brand nostalgia which influenced the taste of the stuff. One might question the validity of using expensive hospital equipment and highly trained medical professionals to explain choices of fizzy drinks with no nutritional value whatsoever— but that would be to get a bit real.

The good news is that all this dubious effort is just as likely to fail as it is to succeed. If an ad can latch on to the emotion of a winning goal in a football match or the tears and triumphs of *Pop Idol* [the British parent of *American Idol*], then there's a good chance it will do the trick. Much else is trial and error. Focus groups assembled to pretest the vibe are notoriously unreliable as they can be suggestible and become dominated by loudmouths.

Anxieties of Influence

One might well ask: so what? So what if silly money . . . pushes the usual goods/junk, if I can still make an informed choice about what I buy?

Well, maybe. . . . But how would you react if all this were seeping into the very pores of the culture you're part of—and changing it? Mass advertising is about brands with the most money behind them pushing to the top. Smaller companies with less of this fluff-muscle don't always survive.

More perniciously, corporate giants try every trick in the book to control our media channels. Much of the mainstream media exists to sell audiences to advertisers. Newspapers aren't profitable based on sales alone. The missing factor is ad money. It's their lifeblood. Teen magazines (especially those aimed at girls) are little more than catalogues for products—and that's the content. The profile of the chubby hero who saved a life is usually tucked away at the end. Here's what an agency representing Coca-Cola demanded in a letter to magazines: 'We believe that positive and upbeat editorial provides a compatible environment in which to communicate the brand's message. . . . We consider the following subjects to be inappropriate and require that our ads are not placed adjacent to articles discussing the following issues: Hard News; Sex related issues; Drugs (Prescription or Illegal); Medicine (eg chronic illnesses such as cancer, diabetes, AIDS, etc); Health (eg mental or physical conditions); Negative Diet Information (eg bulimia, anorexia, quick weight loss, etc); Food; Political issues; Environmental issues; Articles containing vulgar language; Religion.' So, not much chance of a mention of the intimidation of union workers in Coke's Colombian plant, or of the charges of water pollution in India, then.

If anyone still thought they were watching 'the news' on CNN, anchor Jack Cafferty's on-air views might disabuse them: 'We are not here as a public service. We're here to make money. We sell advertising, and we do it on the premise that people are going to watch. If you don't cover the miners because you want to do a story about a debt crisis in Brazil at the time everybody else is covering the miners, then Citibank calls up and says, "You know what? We're not renewing the commercial contract." I mean, it's a business. In the US, one study found that 40 per cent of the 'news' content of a typical newspaper originated in press releases, story memos and suggestions from PR companies.

Hungry for Cool

More subtle is the cultural shift wrought in the media—light, non-political television programming that contributes to a 'buying mood'; magazines filled with little nuggets of 'instant gratification'; serious newspapers that insert lengthy travel and fashion sections for no obvious reason. So much happiness, so unbearable. Advertising consistently portrays 'lifestyles' that are beyond the reach of all but the wealthy. This is somehow viewed as 'apolitical'. Yet charities' ads calling for dropping Southern debt or opposing cruelty to animals often fall foul of regulators or media ad-sales teams for being 'too political'.

As a child I loved the ads before the movie. They were zippy and bright. I found the varied angles they took before the 'Ta-dahhh!' moment when the product was plugged ingenious. I still find the creative energy that goes into them intriguing, but feel tired by their consistently conservative values and know better about the social, economic and environmental issues behind the products they push. I also feel fed up by the sheer volume of the glitzy deluge. Corporate advertisers know this fed up feeling all too well and have responded with marketing moves that look less like traditional advertising but seep more than ever into our lives. The upshot is that everything gets branded, logo-ed or sponsored. Supermarkets that shaft farmers sponsor children's play areas and school computers. Children are employed to hand out freebies to other kids and talk them up ('peer marketing'). Conspicuous charity abounds, trying to make the brand look more benign—for example, Ronald McDonald House offers accommodation to families with sick children. Product placement sneaks into movies, TV shows, computer games and even novels. Our email and cell phones are bombarded. Most websites would collapse without revenue from ads that get ever more lively and mysterious.

With traditional advertising showing diminishing returns, corporations get into all sorts of contortions. The apparel company Diesel ran a multimillion-dollar campaign contrasting clothing ads with scenes of hardship in North Korea; Benetton notoriously used the image of a man dying of AIDS to push its duds. Wow, just feel that edge!

Advertising and the Transformation of Desire

A certain amount of advertising is probably unavoidable—indeed, countries that curb it often flood mental spaces with political propaganda instead. But the worldview the ad biz pushes is so out of touch with real life that it can mess up our heads. Ever wondered where that urge to shop when you're feeling a bit down comes from? Or how our desire for social change or rebellion gets transformed into speed, sex, indulgence and living for the moment? Why is so much of our culture about dictating taste (the tyrannies of 'cool') and transforming it into want? Why are disadvantaged groups (be they dark-skinned, sexual minorities, people with disabilities, you name it) so absent from this trendy world, unless they are being fetishized by niche marketing?

With the deluge comes avoidance. Ungrateful wretches that we are, we try to block out as much as we can. TV advertising is in crisis. Ad guru Lord Saatchi thinks young people nowadays have 'continual partial attention'—the kind of brain that's constantly sifting but records little. His answer is for companies to strive for 'one-word equity' to fit this goldfish attention span—Be™, Live™, Buy™, anyone?

This dizziness is reflected in the philosophical musings of Maurice Lévy, top honcho of advertising giant Publicis: 'Consumers do not want only to be given an astonishingly wide-ranging choice. They want that choice to be renewed at intervals that are always shorter. This is the reason why we have to redefine our very notion of time. What we have to deal with is not only change, but an acceleration of change itself. Not only transformations, but the transformation of transformations: it will be a real challenge to make fidelity out of inconstancy.'

He doesn't stop to ponder how his work is all about creating this blur of inconstancy. Advertising's influence is being implicated in eating, compulsive and attention-deficit disorders. In the Majority World the big brand steamroller is intent on creating Westernized aspirational cultures often at odds with local cultures. If we are to free identity from consumerism, reality checks are our strongest weapon. If struck by an ad, it's useful to measure how much of it is actually telling you something about the product and how much is image. Brands are eager that you identify with them, make them a part of your lives—deny them that privilege. Independent media (like the *NI* [*New Internationalist.*] There's quite a bit of ad-industry nervousness as brands come under attack and marketing tactics backfire. Could the industry one day start to tell us things we actually want to know? The distorting mirror will need to shatter first before a floating world comes into view.

The Culture of Consumption May Cause Psychological Harm

Michael McCarthy

Michael McCarthy is the North American editor for the British medical journal the Lancet. *In the following article, McCarthy reports on the views of the psychologist Allen Kanner and others that the culture of consumption is doing great psychological harm yet being ignored by most American psychologists. According to McCarthy, Kanner says that mainstream psychology has overlooked the ill effects of consumerism because it is not perceived as a problem of the individual, because there is a social taboo against criticizing U.S. capitalism, and because the profession of psychology has been deeply involved in the creation of the consumer culture of today. Kanner and his colleagues seek to show that consumerism is worthy of psychologists' attention and to encourage debate within their profession over the effects that consumerism and materialism are having on individuals and society. But other psychologists, McCarthy reports, deny Kanner's claim and argue that it is just a thinly disguised attack on capitalism and that there are in fact healthy motives for acquiring wealth.*

C an psychology save us from our lust for possessions?

A culture of consumption, which exalts the acquisition of material goods over almost all other values, is causing severe psychological harm yet it is ignored by the psychology profession, argues a group of psychologists in a new book.

The collection of essays called *Psychology and Consumer Culture: The Struggle for a Good Life in a Materialistic World* was edited by Allen Kanner, a child and family psychologist who practises in the San Francisco area of California, USA, and Tim Kasser, a professor of psychology at Knox College in Galesburg, Illinois.

"Consumerism is one of the most important psychological issues of our times", Kanner said in a telephone interview, "but it is getting scant attention."

Kanner says there are three main reasons why mainstream psychology has not looked seriously at consumerism. First, he says, the profession prefers to deal with problems on the level of the individual. "The tendency is to focus on individuals, families, and small groups", not culture, he says.

Books on child development, he notes, are "all about relationships with family and maybe peers", but there is no mention of the effect that television and advertising have on a child's development, even though a child in the USA watches on average 4 hours of television a day.

Second, "there is a social taboo against criticising capitalism in the USA that prevents psychologists from objectively looking at the harm that is being done" by the current economic and social system, Kanner says. "It's subtle but it's there."

And, finally, the profession of psychology has been deeply involved in the creation of the consumer culture of today—in particular by helping to create modern marketing techniques.

Tim Kasser says another obstacle is the emphasis of US psychology on behavioural and cognitive approaches, which, he says, focus on helping people adapt to society so they can feel at ease, function better, and succeed in society. "From that theoretical viewpoint there would be no reason to critique our consumer society", Kasser argues.

To make the case that consumerism is worthy of psychology's attention, Kasser and others have been applying the methods used to study disorders such as depression and anxiety to assess the relation between the importance that people place on material values and their sense of happiness and well-being.

"The basic finding is that people who orient their lives in pursuit of the goals that consumer society tells us to pursue are less happy", Kasser says.

"To be happy people need to feel safe and secure", he says, "they need to feel competent and able to do the things they need to do; they need to feel they are connected to people, loved; and they need to feel free, autonomous.

"These are values you do not see advertised very much in society, except as a way to sell something else", Kasser says.

A good example, he says, are the advertisements for sport utility vehicles, the popular four-wheel drive trucks known as SUVs that have replaced many of the smaller, more efficient family cars in the USA.

"Look at the ads. Why do you buy an SUV? Because they're safe, because they're so big. Why do you buy an SUV? Because it shows you've made it, that you're competent. Why do you buy an SUV? Because people will love you. Why do you buy an SUV? Because it makes you free, you can go anywhere."

"Advertisers are no dummies", Kasser adds, "they know what they're doing."

But despite such promises, Kasser says, most research shows that people who place a high value on attaining financial success, having nice possessions, and having the right image and high status based on wealth and possessions score lower on several measures of well-being.

Compared with people who prize "intrinsic" values such as personal development, family relationships, and community involvement, people who are materialistic, he says, "report less happiness, less satisfaction with life, less feeling of vitality, lower energy, and fewer experiences with emotions like happiness and contentment. And they report more problems with depression, anxiety, and alcohol and tobacco use."

Conversely, people who place a higher value on things such as self-knowledge, family, and friendships "are happier, have higher quality relationships, and a greater sense of freedom", Kasser says.

However, not everyone agrees with Kasser and Kanner's analysis. Edwin A Locke, an industrial psychologist and emeritus professor of leadership and motivation at the R H Smith School of Business at the University of Maryland (College Park, MD), says such arguments are really just thinly disguised attacks on capitalism.

"The desire for material things is associated with poor mental health only when it is associated with certain motives: with the desire for power, in other words 'lording it over' others; a desire to show off, in other words 'conspicuous consumption'; or a desire to prove yourself, to show that you're not as stupid as everyone says you are. These motives are all rooted in self-doubt."

There are, in fact, many healthy motives for acquiring wealth, Locke says: the desire for financial security, to provide for your family and your children's education, "to enjoy a comfortable life", and "to buy goods you personally enjoy".

"It's not the desire for goods as such that is bad for people, but it's desiring them for the wrong reasons", he says.

Locke also is not convinced that advertising has as great an effect as some people say. "If ads were so powerful we'd all be robots and companies would all be rich. But companies go broke all the time and advertisers fail because people choose not to buy their goods."

But some people are more vulnerable to the materialistic appeals than others, says Kasser—in particular people who come from poorer backgrounds, from broken homes with divorced parents, and families in which the parent or parents were cold and controlling. These people are insecure and want to feel secure, Kasser says, and society, through advertising, tells them, "If you want to feel secure, buy this, become rich, and so they latch on to materialistic values as a way to feel good about themselves."

"Material things may help you feel good—or I guess I would say they help you not feel bad for a little while. But they don't do anything to solve the underlying problem."

Kanner and Kasser hope their book will encourage debate within their profession over the effects that consumerism and materialism are having on individuals and society.

Kasser feels that work over the past 10 years has established the "epidemiology" of materialism. "The evidence that materialism is associated with lower personal well-being is very good." The task now is to look for remedies. Kasser thinks the problem will require attacks on several levels. As much as possible, people have to be protected from exposure to commercial messages by the creation of commercial-free zones, he says. People need to be inoculated against the influence of media and advertising by being given media training to help them resist. And people need to be given support so they can stick to their values. "People feel that personal growth, their family, and their community are important to them, but they feel they can't structure their lives so that they can actually live their values." Such support would include reforms that, for example, shortened the working week to 35 or even 30 hours.

Finally, Kasser says, we need to overcome the belief that economic growth will improve the quality of our lives. "All the data show that, since the 1950s, as our economy has grown, happiness hasn't changed at all—and other things like depression and anxiety have all gone up", Kasser says. "We're rich enough—so more wealth is not going to make us happier . . . it's about improving other aspects of our world."

But what are the chances of any this coming about? Allen Kanner admits it seems quixotic. But he likens the current situation of the anticonsumerism movement to the early days of the civil rights, women's rights, or gay rights movements. In each case people thought these problems were just the way things were and certainly not problems within the scope of psychology. But within a short time, as people became aware of the issues, there was an explosion of research on the effects that racism, sexism, and homophobia had on both individuals and society.

The trick, says Kanner, is to make sure that when the profession finally does turn its attention to consumerism and materialism it does not define it primarily as a personal problem. "It should frame the problem as an interface between the personal, social, and political."

"We're not going to change this one person at a time," Kanner says. "There has to be systemic changes before it's going to get better—but the profession doesn't want to go there."

CHAPTER 3

Consumerism and the Global Economy

Turning the Poor into Consumers Is Not the Answer to Poverty

Vandana Shiva

Vandana Shiva is a physicist, ecologist, activist, editor, and author. In India she has established Navdanya, a movement for biodiversity conservation and farmers' rights. She also directs the Research Foundation for Science, Technology and Natural Resource Policy. In the following article, she counters the view of Jeffrey Sachs, a Columbia University economist, who argues that the world's poor, particularly in the developing world, have been "left behind" while others have enjoyed the fruits of the industrial revolution. Shiva says it is wrong to equate poverty with lack of participation in the global market economy and argues further that those who are poor have become so because they are denied access to their own wealth and resources. The answer to poverty is not "growth," she says, and the poor need not be given access to consumer goods in order to be wealthy.

The cover story of the *Time Magazine* of March 14, 2005 was dedicated to the theme, "How to End Poverty". It was based on an essay by Jeffrey Sachs, "The End of Poverty", from his book with the same title. The photos accompanying the essay are homeless children, scavengers in garbage dumps, heroin addicts. These are images of disposable people, people whose lives, resources, livelihoods have been snatched from them by a brutal, unjust, excluding process which generates poverty for the majority and prosperity for a few.

Garbage is the waste of a throwaway society—ecological societies have never had garbage. Homeless children are the consequences of impoverishment of communities and families

Vandana Shiva, "How to End Poverty: Making Poverty History and the History of Poverty," *Zmag*, May 11, 2005. © 2005 Zmag.org. Reproduced by permission of the author.

who have lost their resources and livelihoods. These are images of the perversion and externalities of a non-sustainable, unjust, inequitable economic growth model.

In *Staying Alive*, I had referred to a book entitled *Poverty: The Wealth of the People* in which an African writer draws a distinction between poverty as subsistence, and misery as deprivation. It is useful to separate a cultural conception of simple, sustainable living as poverty from the material experience of poverty that is a result of dispossession and deprivation.

Culturally Perceived Poverty vs. Real Poverty

Culturally perceived poverty need not be real material poverty: sustenance economies, which satisfy basic needs through self-provisioning, are not poor in the sense of being deprived. Yet the ideology of development declares them so because they do not participate overwhelmingly in the market economy, and do not consume commodities produced for and distributed through the market even though they might be satisfying those needs through self-provisioning mechanisms.

People are perceived as poor if they eat millets (grown by women) rather than commercially produced and distributed processed junk foods sold by global agribusiness. They are seen as poor if they live in self-built housing made from ecologically adapted natural material like bamboo and mud rather than in cement houses. They are seen as poor if they wear handmade garments of natural fibre rather than synthetics.

Sustenance, as culturally perceived poverty, does not necessarily imply a low physical quality of life. On the contrary, because sustenance economies contribute to the growth of nature's economy and the social economy, they ensure a high quality of life measure in terms of right to food and water, sustainability of livelihoods, and robust social and cultural identity and meaning.

On the other hand, the poverty of the 1 billion hungry and the 1 billion malnutritioned people who are victims of obesity suffer from both cultural and material poverty. A system that creates denial and disease, while accumulating trillions of dollars of super profits for agribusiness, is a system for creating poverty for people. Poverty is a final state, not an initial state of an economic paradigm, which destroys ecological and social systems for maintaining life, health and sustenance of the planet and people.

Other Forms of Poverty

And economic poverty is only one form of poverty. Cultural poverty, social poverty, ethical poverty, ecological poverty, spiritual poverty are other forms of poverty more prevalent in the so-called rich North than in the so-called poor South. And those other poverties cannot be overcome by dollars. They need compassion and justice, caring and sharing.

Ending poverty requires knowing how poverty is created. However, Jeffrey Sachs views poverty as the original sin. As he declares:

> A few generations ago, almost everybody was poor. The Industrial Revolution led to new riches, but much of the world was left far behind.

This is totally false history of poverty, and cannot be the basis of making poverty history. Jeffrey Sachs has got it wrong. The poor are not those who were left behind, they are the ones who were pushed out and excluded from access to their own wealth and resources.

The "poor are not poor because they are lazy or their governments are corrupt." They are poor because their wealth has been appropriated and wealth-creating capacity destroyed. The riches accumulated by Europe were based on riches appropriated from Asia, Africa and Latin America. Without the destruction of India's rich textile industry, without the take over of the spice trade, without the genocide of the native American tribes, without Africa's slavery, the industrial revolution would not have led to new riches for Europe or the U.S. It was the violent take over of Third World resources and Third World markets that created wealth in the North—but it simultaneously created poverty in the South.

Affluence and Poverty Are Linked

Two economic myths facilitate a separation between two intimately linked processes: the growth of affluence and the growth of poverty. Firstly, growth is viewed only as growth of capital. What goes unperceived is the destruction in nature and in people's sustenance economy that this growth creates. The two simultaneously created 'externalities' of growth—environmental destruction and poverty creation—are then causally linked, not to the processes of growth, but to each other. Poverty, it is stated, causes environmental destruction. The disease is then offered as a cure: growth will solve the problems of poverty and environmental crisis it has given rise to in the first place. This is the message of Jeffrey Sachs' analysis.

The second myth that separates affluence from poverty, is the assumption that if you produce what you consume, you do not produce. This is the basis on which the production boundary is drawn for national accounting that measures economic growth. Both myths contribute to the mystification of growth and consumerism, but they also hide the real processes that create poverty.

First, the market economy dominated by capital is not the only economy; development has, however, been based on the growth of the market economy. The invisible costs of development have been the destruction of two other economies: nature's processes and people's survival. The ignorance or neglect of these two vital economies is the reason why development has posed a threat of ecological destruction and a threat to human survival, both of which, however, have remained 'hidden negative externalities' of the development process.

Instead of being seen as results of exclusion, they are presented as "those left behind". Instead of being viewed as those who suffer the worst burden of unjust growth in the form of poverty, they are falsely presented as those not touched by growth. This false separation of processes that create affluence from those that create poverty is at the core of Jeffrey Sachs' analysis. His recipes will therefore aggravate and deepen poverty instead of ending it.

Elevation of the Market at the Expense of Ecology

Trade and exchange of goods and services have always existed in human societies, but these were subjected to nature's and people's economies. The elevation of the domain of the market and man-made capital to the position of the highest organizing principle for societies has led to the neglect and destruction of the other two organizing principles—ecology and survival—which maintain and sustain life in nature and society.

Modern economies and concepts of development cover only a negligible part of the history of human interaction with nature. For centuries, principles of sustenance have given human societies the material basis of survival by deriving livelihoods directly from nature through self-provisioning mechanisms. Limits in nature have been respected and have guided the limits of human consumption. In most countries of the South large numbers of people continue to derive their sustenance in the survival economy which remains invisible to market-oriented development.

All people in all societies depend on nature's economy for survival. When the organizing principle for society's relationship with nature is sustenance, nature exists as a commons. It becomes a resource when profits and accumulation become the organizing principles and create an imperative for the exploitation of resources for the market.

Without clean water, fertile soils and crop and plant genetic diversity, human survival is not possible. These commons have been destroyed by economic development, resulting in the creation of a new contradiction between the economy of natural processes and the survival economy, because those people deprived of their traditional land and means of survival by development are forced to survive on an increasingly eroded nature.

Preventing Access to Their Own Wealth

People do not die for lack of incomes. They die for lack of access to resources. Here too Jeffrey Sachs is wrong when he says, "In a world of plenty, 1 billion people are so poor, their lives are in danger." The indigenous people in the Amazon, the mountain communities in the Himalaya, peasants whose land has not been appropriated and whose water and biodiversity have not been destroyed by debt-creating industrial agriculture are ecologically rich, even though they do not earn a dollar a day.

On the other hand, even at five dollars a day, people are poor if they have to buy their basic needs at high prices. Indian peasants who have been made poor and pushed into debt over the past decade to create markets for costly seeds and agrichemicals through economic globalisation are ending their lives in the thousands.

When seeds are patented and peasants will pay $1 trillion in royalties, they will be $1 trillion poorer. Patents on medicines increase costs of AIDS drugs from $200 to $20,000, and cancer drugs from $2,400 to $36,000 for a year's treatment. When water is privatized, and global corporations make $1 trillion from commodification of water, the poor are poorer by $1 trillion.

The movements against economic globalisation and maldevelopment are movements to end poverty by ending the exclusions, injustices and ecological non-sustainability that are the root causes of poverty.

The $50 billion of "aid" North to South is a tenth of the $500 billion flow South to North as interest payments and other unjust mechanisms in the global economy imposed by World Bank, IMF [International Monetary Fund]. With privatization of essential services and an unfair globalisation imposed through W.T.O. [World Trade Organization], the poor are being made poorer.

Indian peasants are losing $26 billion annually just in falling farm prices because of dumping and trade liberalisation. As a result of unfair, unjust globalisation, which is leading to corporate take over of food and water. More than $5 trillion will be transferred from poor people to rich countries just for food and water. The poor are financing the rich. If we are serious about ending poverty, we have to be serious about ending the unjust and violent systems for wealth creation which create poverty by robbing the poor of their resources, livelihoods and incomes.

Jeffrey Sachs deliberately ignores this "taking," and only addresses "giving," which is a mere 0.1% of the "taking" by the North. Ending poverty is more a matter of taking less than giving an insignificant amount more. Making poverty history needs getting the history of poverty right. And Sachs has got it completely wrong.

Consumerism in Japan's Stagnant Economy

Victoria James

Victoria James has written for the New Statesman *and the* Japan Times. *In the following article, she describes how a prolonged economic downturn in Japan affected, and was affected by, consumerism. Some Japanese continued to buy expensive luxuries, while saving on basic goods at newly popular low-end stores. Others responded to the economic troubles, however, by saving their money, causing problems for an economy that had relied on consumer spending in the past.*

"My God," muttered the friend beside me, "it's like Agincourt [popular UK nightclub]." Opposite, just metres away, waited a mass of people, ten deep. At a given signal, we would rush towards each other, clash and trample. Some might even fall, toppling from their platform boots to graze sunbed-tanned knees unprotected by micro skirts.

Welcome to Hachiko crossing at the heart of Tokyo's Shibuya, the favourite shopping district of Japan's trendy young citizens. Whatever you've read in the papers about Japan's economic downturn, consumer carnage takes place here most weekday evenings, and all day on Saturday and Sunday.

Over in Ginza—where skirts are longer, heels lower, and both generally bear a designer logo—things look much the same. At weekends, the central avenues are closed to vehicles and the streets full of shoppers. You have to wait to get into the new Louis Vuitton store, 1,230 square metres of branded luxury, where the cheapest item is a £170 business-card holder and the average spend is £430. The queues will probably be even longer at the Hermes store ... occupy[ing] 2,025 square metres of prime Ginza space. . . .

This is what the Japanese recession looks like.

Reasons for Recession

I didn't need an expert to tell me that "Tokyo's huge crowds of young people are bonded to conspicuous consumption and so skew the [economic] picture", but one did anyway. Aaron Cohen, the former chief financial economist for the Daiwa Securities Group, believes that the roots of the country's financial crisis lie deep below the surface indicators of consumer behaviour, faltering stocks and fluctuating yen.

In his view, the causes of the recession can be traced through decades of economic mismanagement, such as the government's "time-honoured practice of pumping money into sectors noted for their political contributions, and calling it 'public spending'". The consequences, including a national debt that is forecast to exceed 220 per cent of GDP [gross national product] by 2005, "will roll over for generations".

The extent of recent media coverage has made amateur economic analysts of us all in Japan. We gloomily discuss the "triple bear" scenario of concurrently falling yen, stocks and bonds. Predictions about the American economy's V-shaped (sharp slowdown followed by swift improvement) or U-shaped recovery (the same, but with a flat period of minimal growth in between) are contrasted with Japan's hapless L-shape (where recession drags on with no upturn in sight). And yet around us, people appear as well dressed and the shops as busy as ever. What kind of a recession is this?

Bargain Stores Are the New Consumer Rave

Back in Ginza, one block down from Louis Vuitton, is the unobtrusive fifth-floor outlet of a business credited with changing the way the Japanese shop. Uniqlo is an unappealing cross between Gap and C&A [a popular UK clothing chain]. Its merchandise and store design ape the former, but with the bargain-basement feel of the latter. In 2000, it almost doubled its previous year's sales and profits.

Cheap stores have enjoyed an increasingly high profile in recent years. The most recent retail phenomenon before Uniqlo was the everything-at-100-yen (about [U.S. 90 cents]) Daiso Plaza, still thriving with 2,000 stores countrywide. What is new about Uniqlo is its success in crossing over into the consumer mainstream. Merchandise in Daiso Plaza is functional and anonymous—kitchen utensils, cheap cosmetics, batteries and cassette tapes. Uniqlo sells only clothing, and the brand is so pervasive that there's no chance of your basic blue polo shirt being mistaken for a Ralph Lauren.

But thrift is no longer something to be ashamed of. The word *gekiyasu* ("super-cheap"), once undesirable in a consumer culture obsessed with exclusivity and expense, is now a quality much touted in advertisements. Designer brands may, ironically, be receiving a boost from the *gekiyasu* trend ("If we want luxury goods we can save up for them by buying Uniqlo," said a 30-year-old Yokahama woman in a recent survey of consumer behaviour). The loser is that symbol not just of Japanese consumerism, but of Japanese society itself: the department store. Five minutes' walk from the heart of Ginza is the deserted shell of Sogo's former Yurakucho store. Sogo went into effective liquidation in [2000], unable to hold its own in the increasingly competitive *depato* [department store] market.

Survivors of the store wars are resorting to various strategies attract customers. Some renovate their premises, hold discreet sales (tastefully disguised as "boutiques" or "speciality fairs") or expand popular basement food departments. One—Mitsukoshi's eight-storey Yokohama branch—opened its gates to the Trojan horse and leased a floor to Uniqlo, causing an immediate upturn in profitability.

What is at stake is not so much the fate of individual stores or retail groups as the very nature of shopping in Japan. Philip Brasor, journalist and trend-watcher, says that "the public has given up on shopping as a social activity". He attributes this to "the public's realisation that it owns all that it will ever want", leading it to "start comparison shopping for the things it actually needs".

Survival vs. Shopping

Despite a record 0.7 per cent drop in retail prices in 2000—a drop that exceeded the two previous years of decline—people are still reluctant to spend. One simple reason is that they have less money. April [2001]'s *Japan Economic Review* estimated the average monthly income for a working family at 452,510 yen (£2,606 [US$5115]), and the average consumption at 307,952 yen (£1,774 [US$3481]); both represent a proportional decrease from the previous month. But where is the rest of the money—about £832 [US$1632]—going?

"We're saving for our old age," was the reply of Japan's then 103-year-old twins Gin-san and Kin-san, when asked [in 1997] what they planned to do with income generated by their centenarian celebrity. Total personal savings in Japan exceed $11trn, the highest in the world, as is the percentage of their income set aside by Japanese savers. Despite an average interest rate of just 0.25 per cent, the Japanese are pathologically prudent.

Businesses, analysts and the government would like to see these piggy banks smashed open. The problem is that Japan's rainy-day savers are far too good at spotting the clouds on the horizon. Job insecurity is widespread. Corporate bankruptcies, no longer rare, endanger pensions accumulated through decades of labour. One consequence of Japan's postwar demographic is that the cautious elderly already far outnumber the free-spending young. Another is that the social security system will have to care for ever more pensioners from the contributions of ever fewer workers. The anxious middle-aged and far-sighted young are hoarding their yen in order to support themselves if the state becomes unable to do so.

Economic Failure

Even though bank and post-office interest rates represent barely more return on your money than stashing cash in a cardboard box under the bed, the Japanese shun other forms of investment. There is no shareholding culture, as in the US, and the recent market crash has confirmed the suspicion with which such risky speculation is widely viewed. Real-estate investment ceased to be attractive after the bubble years, since when land prices have been in ceaseless free fall. . . .

The comedown from the asset-inflated Eighties turned business balance sheets red, due not necessarily to failing performance, but to rapidly devaluing real-estate investments. Individual homeowners found themselves mired in negative equity, with properties worth less than the loan taken out to part-pay for them. Finally, with what Aaron Cohen calls the "banking debacle" of institutional failures from 1997 onwards, even this last safe place for savings was threatened. Opting for a more secure version of the cardboard box, anxious Japanese made the home safe, complete with burglar-proof combination lock, the surprise consumer hit of 1999 and 2000.

The whole system generates an endless downward spiral. One simplified sequence works as follows: falling land prices endanger corporate viability, which threatens jobs, causing retrenchment of personal expenditure, thereby creating further price deflation. Other strands involve stock and bond performance, Japan's international standing and the strength of overseas competition. The shape of Japan's "deflation"—acknowledged as such for the first time since the Second World War . . .—is not so much a single spiral as a DNA-like helix of interwoven chains of cause and effect. All however, tend inexorably downwards. . . .

Leaders Hope to Fix Japan's Economy

The election ... of the reform-minded Junichiro Koizumi as president of the ruling Liberal Democratic Party, and thus to the office of prime minister, gave business chiefs the leader they wanted.

The popular approval rating of Koizumi's new cabinet, more than 86 per cent by reliable estimates, makes even [UK prime minister Tony] Blair's 1998 honeymoon look passionless. But Koizumi's pet projects of post-office privatisation and reform of Japan's parliamentary system hardly represent decisive action on the economy. True, his newly appointed finance minister is younger than the previous office holder but, at the age of 79, Masajuro Shiokawa is more old guard than new broom.

External observers look for the application of cold steel not as a sword to slice through the knot, but as a scalpel to cut away the long ingrowing sickness of Japan's economic structure. The *South China Morning Post* has compared Japan to "a patient who denies the seriousness of his complaint until it becomes a matter of life and death ... [now] willing to submit to the scalpel of the iconoclastic new prime minister, Junichiro Koizumi". The prognosis is not good: "Koizumi has been called in ... after the usual medicine has failed. He will have to be something of a miracle worker to effect a cure."

Aaron Cohen is equally sceptical: "Think of the saying 'The operation was a success, but the patient died'. Surgically dealing with the financial sector is likely to have serious side effects."

We should make no mistake, however. Japan remains the world's second-largest economy, the most generous donator of overseas development aid, and, as acknowledged by other east Asian nations, the hinge of that region's return to prosperity. The patient's full recovery matters to us all.

Charitable Consumerism Is Flawed

Julie Hollar

Julie Hollar is a writer and film director and the former communications director for Fairness and Accuracy in Reporting. In the following article, she discusses the reporting on news about Africa in the U.S. media, pointing out that it is most often presented through the lens of Western celebrities. These celebrities, such as the singer Bono and the actor Leonardo DeCaprio, make Africa "sexy," and she argues that news coverage about Africa has increased not because of public interest in serious stories coming from the continent but because of the thirst for information about the lives of the rich and famous. Just as many Americans consume information about their favorite stars, those stars' humanitarian relief efforts in Africa are packaged as a commodity. Some celebrities have also launched products to draw attention to their chosen causes in Africa, but Hollar questions the idea of using Western consumerism to defend Africans and criticizes consumption-based solutions as naïve and short sighted.

"Africa is sexy and people need to know that," declared U2 singer Bono, promoting his new (RED) line of products that propose to save Africa one iPod at a time.

Celebrity interest in Africa is not particularly new, but today more stars than ever seem to be converging upon the continent, with television crews seldom far behind. But, as Bono clearly understands, what media tend to find sexy about Africa is not Africa itself, but the stars like himself who have taken up causes in the region. In television news in particular, with its typically cursory treatment of subjects and emphasis on the visual, African countries and issues are to a striking degree seen through the prism of celebrity.

Julie Hollar, "Bono, I Presume?: Covering Africa Through Celebrities," *FAIR*, May 2007. Reproduced by permission.

Diamonds and DiCaprio

When *Blood Diamond*, a Hollywood film starring Leonardo DiCaprio, was released in theaters [in 2006], it prompted a brief spike in news coverage of Sierra Leone's recent bloody civil war and the role of diamond smuggling in its funding. In just one week, Sierra Leone's history of "conflict diamonds" was mentioned 11 times on the news programs of ABC, CBS and NBC. In comparison, during the entire length of the country's civil war, which lasted from 1991 to 2002, the central role of diamonds in the conflict came up a grand total of 26 times—an average of just over twice a year.

For stories about Africa, this kind of celebrity coverage is par for the course. In fact, [from 2005 to 2007], the networks mentioned Sierra Leone only 24 times, and besides the 11 mentions that concerned *Blood Diamond*, one was a story about actor Angelina Jolie, one was about musician Kanye West, and two involved actor Isaiah Washington—meaning nearly two-thirds of the network news coverage Sierra Leone received in those two years was generated by U.S. celebrities.

Though several of the *Blood Diamond*–tied segments did briefly explain the past and current problems surrounding conflict diamonds, few delved deeper. For soundbites, most didn't look past DiCaprio and his fellow cast and crew on the one side, or a representative from the diamond industry on the other; only three of the 11 stories included outside expert perspectives on the issue, including one extensive interview with an Africa policy expert from World Vision, a Christian humanitarian organization involved in conflict diamond work. Besides *Blood Diamond* star Djimon Hounsou, a U.S. citizen originally from Benin, not a single African source was interviewed in any of the segments.

Hounsou tried to focus media attention on the ongoing issue of child soldiers at three different points in an interview on NBC's *Saturday Today*, but each time anchor Campbell Brown diverted the conversation, taking Hounsou back to the favored media storylines of the movie itself and the diamond industry's PR [public relations] counteroffensive.

It's hard to say how much of the *Blood Diamond* coverage would have actually addressed the issue of conflict diamonds themselves had the diamond industry not launched a multi-million-dollar damage-control PR campaign in response to the film's release, giving the media a fight to cover rather than just another story about bad news from Africa. When Kanye West remixed his song "Diamonds Are Forever" as a protest against the diamond industry's abuses in Africa, it failed to register on the networks; the one pre–*Blood Diamond* network mention of his song did not even note its political message.

Madonna in Malawi

Just a few months earlier, pop star Madonna's adoption of a child from Malawi set off an even bigger firestorm of news coverage, prolonged by Malawian civil rights groups' challenge to the adoption and questions around whether the star skirted Malawi's laws governing foreign adoptions. The networks returned to the story 38 times, which constituted their only mentions of Malawi the entire year, and more than two-thirds of the coverage they've devoted to the poverty-stricken country [from 2001 to 2007].

During that time, Malawi suffered from two devastating famines for which the United Nations and aid agencies issued dire warnings and urgent pleas for aid; on October 15, 2005, the Malawian president declared the entire country a disaster zone. The two famines combined received a total of six mentions on the networks during those years—one of which led with a mention of rock star Bono's trip there with then–U.S. Treasury Secretary Paul O'Neill.

In an interview on NBC's *Dateline*, Madonna mused, "All the criticism is ultimately a blessing in disguise because now people know about Malawi, and now people know about the orphanage there." On NBC's *Today* show, anchor Matt Lauer agreed: "The one thing you have to say, a lot of people before this didn't know what Malawi was. And at least they're talking about the situation there now."

But what have TV viewers really learned about Malawi? Those newscasts that looked at all beyond Madonna to the circumstances in the country did not stray far from generalizations like "poverty, hunger and disease"—which is what most Americans have already heard repeatedly from the media about most of Africa anyway. Not one of the stories on Madonna's adoption even mentioned the recent famines, which, combined with the AIDS crisis (noted by 11—fewer than a third—of the Madonna stories), have been a major cause of the swelling orphanages; an exploration of the deeper roots, like exploitative Western trade and aid policies, was completely off the media agenda. While the networks turned five different times to entertainment reporters from *People*, *US Weekly* and Sky News, only once was a Malawian civil rights leader heard from.

Ultimately, the media frenzy merely reinforced the American public's perception of Africa as a helpless, depressing continent full of children in need of charity. The entire story revolved around that concept of charity, and the debate over Madonna's action was framed as a question of whether she should have taken the child from Malawi or simply given the child's father—who was still alive and in the picture—money to support him there; to question what would need to be done beyond band-aid solutions never seemed to cross journalists' minds. Then again, if Lauer's take is any indication, they seemed to be proud enough that they had even mentioned the word Malawi on air.

Nightly News Notables

Many of those Madonna and *Blood Diamond* segments appeared on the networks' morning or daytime shows, which have traditionally been somewhat "lighter," but celebrity hooks have even penetrated the supposedly more sober and substantive evening newscasts.

Africa-based stories are none too common on the networks' evening newscasts to begin with. In 2006, all three networks combined aired a total of 114 stories with a sub-Saharan African country, region or citizen as a primary subject (43 on ABC, 39 on NBC and 32 on CBS). In 2005 the numbers were even lower, with a total of only 85 stories across the three networks; once again, ABC led (with 31 stories), with NBC close behind (30) and CBS trailing (24).

These counts include lengthier segments as well as shorter headline-type briefs read by anchors, yet the numbers still come up well shy of even a single mention of Africa per network per week. According to media researcher Andrew Tyndall, in 2005 that Africa coverage totaled less than one-half of a percent of newscast time.

With the attention paid to Africa so scant to begin with, it's remarkable that of those 199 Africa stories [from 2005 to 2007], 31—more than 15 percent—came packaged with a celebrity angle.

Leading the charge is *NBC Nightly News*, which contributed more than half of those celebrity stories. Of the show's 70 Africa-related segments, 18 featured celebrities—that's a quarter of *NBC Nightly News* Africa coverage. Many of those focused on Bono, with whom NBC anchor Brian Williams traveled to Africa in May 2006, a trip that generated seven stories, six of which prominently featured the rock star. Bono also figured prominently in NBC's coverage of the Live 8 concerts and other celebrity activism around the G8 [eight economically leading nations] meeting in 2005, which generated six stories that year.

ABC and CBS also managed to work star hooks into some of their slim Africa coverage: Celebs could be found in eight of ABC's 74 stories and five of CBS's 56 stories. In 2005, all such stories involved the G8 celebrity activism, while in 2006 the two networks featured *Blood Diamond*, Madonna and Bono, as well as George Clooney's Darfur activism.

Live 8 Love-In

One might argue that the huge Live 8 concerts were legitimate stories to be told. What's much harder to justify is that the celebrity-studded shows were the second-most-reported Africa story on the evening news that year; those 14 segments were only barely edged out by the 15 pieces broadcast on the crisis in Sudan.

And Live 8 coverage was scarcely about Africa at all; the concerts might have offered a useful springboard from which television news could have explored the G8's economic policies that have kept most African nations mired in poverty, but media seemed happy to keep the focus on the celebrities—most prominently Bono and UK singer Bob Geldof—who did nothing to force the issue, since they seem to count the political leaders as allies who just need a little coaxing at times.

In fact, in an ABC interview, Bono sang Bush's praises: "Remember today that this president committed to try and get all African kids into school. . . . Bill Clinton did an incredible thing on starting this debt cancellation. He deserves real credit. And now, President Bush deserves credit for finishing it out." When NBC asked Geldof if he thought Bush "got" that lifting Africa out of poverty was important, the singer responded: "Yes, I do, actually. You know, I know it's weird, but I think he does."

Meanwhile, besides brief clips of various other musicians and performances, viewers got mostly one-line generalizations about organizers "raising the awareness of African poverty and pressuring world leaders to do something about it" (CBS) or wanting "aid doubled and better trade deals for Africa" (NBC), with the occasional longer laundry list of demands: "Complete debt relief for the world's poorest countries, and a firm commitment of long-term funding to combat famine; the deficits in education, training and security that keep the poor poor; and epidemics, starting with AIDS" (NBC).

While TV cameras trained on Bono and Geldof transmitted messages of praise and declarations that the concerts and the G8 were a tremendous success for Africa, African leaders and activists ignored by the celeb-happy media were soon lamenting the G8 outcomes as a game of smoke and mirrors, and a near-complete failure. Within weeks of the summit, it was revealed that most of the promises made—which hadn't fulfilled the demands of activists in the first place—were quickly being dismantled or were false to begin with.

For example, the debt money and the aid money announced at the close of the summit, which were understood to be separate, turned out to be one and the same, meaning half as much money was being put towards Africa as had been promised. And the touted 100 percent debt relief for several countries turned out to be committed only for the following three years. No changes in the heavily imbalanced trade playing field were enacted (*London Guardian*). And the list goes on.

Africa Action called the G8 a "stunning failure," and the World Development Movement called it a "disaster for the world's poor." Demba Moussa Dembele of the African Forum on Alternatives said (Institute for Public Accuracy): "We feel betrayed by the political messages championed by the celebrity leadership of Live 8 and Make Poverty History. We believe that their demands have failed to confront the underlying causes of poverty and injustice."

Africa Action later pointed out that before the G8 summit, African countries owed a combined total of $15 billion a year on debt payments; after the vaunted debt relief agreements, they owed $14 billion a year. Only a quarter of African countries were even eligible for the debt relief program, which required them to enact harmful neoliberal economic stipulations, like privatization of vital services such as water and education, and acceptance of heavily unequal trade rules that prevent true economic development. What's more, none of them actually received 100 percent debt cancellation.

The G8 summit was an important, and largely disappointing, moment for African countries, but for American TV audiences it played as a feel-good series of concerts with a happy ending.

Leveraging Star Power

It was in the shadow of that media-created myth that NBC anchor Brian Williams traveled to Africa under Bono's wing in May 2006 to report on how "he's leveraging his star power to help the poor and the powerless." Indeed, much of Williams' Africa tour played more like hero-worship than reporting: "He boldly convinced the eight wealthiest nations to forgive massive African debt, and he's successfully lobbied President Bush for billions"; "Because Bono was able to relieve Ghana of debt to richer nations, the clinic is out of debt now and offering more service"; Bono "has leveraged his own name to open doors, raise money and heal what ails an entire continent."

Perhaps unsurprisingly, Bono himself served as Williams' primary source in most of the segments. A few soundbites came from mostly unnamed African citizens, while all of the "expert" sources in Williams' story were Westerners offering thoughts primarily about Bono rather than about Africa; the U.K.'s Gordon Brown talked about how Bono "inspires", the Global Fund director praised Bono's "tough-love approach," and Christian author Rick Warren raved, "I love the way that he's leveraging the fame that he has for good."

Williams didn't bother to speak on camera to a single African expert while visiting the continent—or anyone, for that matter, who might have cast doubt upon Bono's humanitarian image or his prescription for "saving" Africa.

In fact, of all the NBC reports on Africa that week, arguably the most substantive was also the only one that didn't come from Williams on location. His colleague Andrea Mitchell, back home in Washington, reported on the failures of G8 leaders to follow through on the aid promises made the year before. Even that report only gave viewers part of the story, presenting debt relief as an unalloyed success, treating only aid and trade as continuing problems. And it continued the Bono love-fest, allowing as his only failure a hint of idealistic naïveté. "Bono has gotten them to cancel 100 percent of their debt from 13 African nations," Mitchell reported, but he "is discovering that political leaders are quicker to make promises than deliver them."

For his part, Bono maintained a diplomatic posture towards those leaders, telling NBC that "sometimes their hearts are open . . . but their wallets are closed."

And it's perhaps little wonder. When Geldof likewise refused to admit failure on his own part or the part of the leaders he supported, columnist George Monbiot (*Guardian*) suggested that the star had joined the ranks of the "tabloid saints" who "appeared to recognize that if they rattled the cages of the powerful, the newspapers upon which their public regard depended would turn against them." And indeed, celebs espousing more cage-rattling causes—like Sean Penn protesting the Iraq War, or Jane Fonda protesting the Vietnam War— often face criticism, rather than adulation, from the news media for their activism.

But if Bono chafes against such limitations, it hardly shows; in any case, he has modeled himself as the ideal media hero, combining ratings-grabbing celebrity power with a cause that offers praise rather than criticism of Bush, and simplistic, often consumption-based solutions.

NBC's Williams gave this description of Bono's stop in Ghana:

A 46-year-old rock star from Ireland stopping at a small kiosk where a woman from Ghana runs her own business selling shares of call time on cell phones. But Bono likes to stop and point out what works on this continent largely because he's plunged himself into so much sadness. At another stop, he visits the Ghana Stock Exchange, not quite the Big Board but a big and burgeoning development here, and they are justifiably proud.

In the same segment, Bono judged Bush to have been "very honest in his business dealings with me, as has Secretary of State Condoleezza Rice. We did an awful lot of work."

Seeing (RED)

In the same vein, Bono helped launch the (RED) line of products in 2006 that would donate a percentage of profits to fighting AIDS and proposed, in his own words (*NBC Nightly News*), "a way of making it easy for people in the shopping malls and main streets all over this great country to get AIDS drugs to Africans who can't afford them. . . . This is using the force of consumerism . . . to defend the world's most vulnerable."

Of course, the very idea of using Western consumerism to defend Africans would be harder to take seriously if the consumerism-driven Western media talked about, say, the way the old iPod or Motorola phone they tossed in favor of their new (RED) one will likely wind up polluting Africa's land, like much of the toxic electronics trash produced by the United States (*Kenya Nation*). Or the way cotton subsidies in the U.S. that make clothing artificially cheap, thus fueling further consumerism, also squeeze African cotton farmers out of the market and out of a living (Oxfam).

But the (RED) concept fit nicely not only with media's preferred economic prescriptions, but also with their bottom line. According to *Advertising Age*, the money spent advertising (RED) products dwarfed the share of profits destined for Africa. Though (RED) disputed *AdAge*'s numbers, it's clear that the campaign has brought in millions for participating companies—and for the media recipients of those advertising dollars.

While viewers are kept up to the minute on Bono's doings in Africa, major events on the continent have gone almost entirely unreported. The chronically media-neglected Democratic Republic of the Congo, where at least 4 million people have died since 1998 in a devastating conflict (*Lancet*), held its first free elections in 40 years in 2006; meanwhile, Zimbabwe under Robert Mugabe increased its slide into chaos and hyperinflation; neither of these were even mentioned once on the networks' nightly newscasts. Former Liberian leader Charles Taylor was seized in 2006 at the request of new President Ellen Johnson-Sirleaf, who launched historic war crimes trials for mass murder, rape and mutilation. This mustered only one brief mention on ABC, as did the Islamist takeover of Mogadishu [Somalia].

Clearly, following Bono to Africa or reporting on conflict diamonds via Leonardo DiCaprio is both easier and more ratings-friendly than sustaining bureaus and teams of reporters on the ground, researching and reporting on both the bad news and the good from Africa. But as networks under corporate profit demands squeeze their news departments tighter and tighter, viewers can in all likelihood expect more and more clips of Madonna videos and Bono sales pitches substituting for real Africa coverage on TV.

CHAPTER 4

Consumerism and the Environment

Land Should Not Be Destroyed in the Name of Freedom and Opportunity

Wendell Berry

Wendell Berry farms in Port Royal, Kentucky, with his family. He is the author of more than thirty books of fiction, essays, and poetry. In the following article, he laments that Americans have sold the country to corporate interests, allowing them through submissiveness and inaction to take over and destroy vast areas of land. Capitalism in the guise of "freedom," he says, has promoted greed as the dominant virtue, and Americans have allowed their country to be pillaged by an Earth-destroying economy justified by progress and profit. He urges Americans to better respect themselves and their dwelling places, to stop seeing the land as a means from which to cheaply extract goods, and to give an absolute priority to caring well for every bit of American land.

We are destroying our country—I mean our country itself, our land. This is a terrible thing to know, but it is not a reason for despair unless we decide to continue the destruction. If we decide to continue the destruction, that will not be because we have no other choice. This destruction is not necessary. It is not inevitable, except that by our submissiveness we make it so.

We Americans are not usually thought to be a submissive people, but of course we are. Why else would we allow our country to be destroyed? Why else would we be rewarding its destroyers? Why else would we all—by proxies we have given to greedy corporations and corrupt politicians—be participating in its destruction? Most of us are still too sane to piss in our own cistern, but we allow others to do so and we reward them for it. We reward them so well, in fact, that those who piss in our cistern are wealthier than the rest of us.

How do we submit? By not being radical enough. Or by not being thorough enough, which is the same thing.

Protecting the Land Without Protecting the People

Since the beginning of the conservation effort in our country, conservationists have too often believed that we could protect the land without protecting the people. This has begun to change, but for a while yet we will have to reckon with the old assumption that we can preserve the natural world by protecting wilderness areas while we neglect or destroy the economic landscapes—the farms and ranches and working forests—and the people who use them. That assumption is understandable in view of the worsening threats to wilderness areas, but it is wrong. If conservationists hope to save even the wild lands and wild creatures, they are going to have to address issues of economy, which is to say issues of the health of the landscapes and the towns and cities where we do our work, and the quality of that work, and the well-being of the people who do the work.

Governments seem to be making the opposite error, believing that the people can be adequately protected without protecting the land. And here I am not talking about parties or party doctrines, but about the dominant political assumption. Sooner or later, governments will have to recognize that if the land does not prosper, nothing else can prosper for very long. We can have no industry or trade or wealth or security if we don't uphold the health of the land and the people and the people's work.

It is merely a fact that the land, here and everywhere, is suffering. We have the "dead zone" in the Gulf of Mexico and undrinkable water to attest to the toxicity of our agriculture. We know that we are carelessly and wastefully logging our forests. We know that soil erosion, air and water pollution, urban sprawl, the proliferation of highways and garbage are making our lives always less pleasant, less healthful, less sustainable, and our dwelling places more ugly.

Desecrating the Land by Extracting Wealth

Nearly forty years ago my state of Kentucky, like other coal-producing states, began an effort to regulate strip mining. While that effort has continued, and has imposed certain requirements of "reclamation," strip mining has become steadily more destructive of the land and the land's future. We are now permitting the destruction of entire mountains and entire watersheds. No war, so far, has done such extensive or such permanent damage. If we know that coal is an exhaustible resource, whereas the forests over it are with proper use inexhaustible, and that strip mining destroys the forest virtually forever, how can we permit this destruction? If we honor at all that fragile creature the topsoil, so long in the making, so miraculously made, so indispensable to all life, how can we destroy it? If we believe, as so many of us profess to do, that the Earth is God's property and is full of His glory, how can we do harm to any part of it?

In Kentucky, as in other unfortunate states, and again at great public cost, we have allowed—in fact we have officially encouraged—the establishment of the confined animal-feeding industry, which exploits and abuses everything involved: the land, the people, the animals, and the consumers. If we love our country, as so many of us profess to do, how can we so desecrate it?

But the economic damage is not confined just to our farms and forests. For the sake of "job creation," in Kentucky, and in other backward states, we have lavished public money on corporations that come in and stay only so long as they can exploit people here more cheaply than elsewhere. The general purpose of the present economy is to exploit, not to foster or conserve.

Look carefully, if you doubt me, at the centers of the larger towns in virtually every part of our country. You will find that they are economically dead or dying. Good buildings that used to house needful, useful, locally owned small businesses of all kinds are now empty or have evolved into junk stores or antique shops. But look at the houses, the churches, the commercial buildings, the courthouse, and you will see that more often than not they are comely and well made. And then go look at the corporate outskirts: the chain stores, the fast-food joints, the food-and-fuel stores that no longer can be called service stations, the motels. Try to find something comely or well made there.

What is the difference? The difference is that the old town centers were built by people who were proud of their place and who realized a particular value in living there. The old buildings look good because they were built by people who respected themselves and wanted the respect of their neighbors. The corporate outskirts, on the contrary, were built by people who manifestly take no pride in the place, see no value in lives lived there, and recognize no neighbors. The only value they see in the place is the money that can be siphoned out of it to more fortunate places—that is, to the wealthier suburbs of the larger cities.

Market Value and the Corporate Hijacking of Communities

Can we actually suppose that we are wasting, polluting, and making ugly this beautiful land for the sake of patriotism and the love of God? Perhaps some of us would like to think so, but in fact this destruction is taking place because we have allowed ourselves to believe, and to live, a mated pair of economic lies: that nothing has a value that is not assigned to it by the market; and that the economic life of our communities can safely be handed over to the great corporations. We citizens have a large responsibility for our delusion and our destructiveness, and I don't want to minimize that. But I don't want to minimize, either, the large responsibility that is borne by government.

It is commonly understood that governments are instituted to provide certain protections that citizens individually cannot provide for themselves. But governments have tended to assume that this responsibility can be fulfilled mainly by the police and the military. They have used their regulatory powers reluctantly and often poorly. Our governments have only occasionally recognized the need of land and people to be protected against economic violence. It is true that economic violence is not always as swift, and is rarely as bloody, as the violence of war, but it can be devastating nonetheless. Acts of economic aggression can destroy a landscape or a community or the center of a town or city, and they routinely do so.

Such damage is justified by its corporate perpetrators and their political abettors in the name of the "free market" and "free enterprise," but this is a freedom that makes greed the dominant economic virtue, and it destroys the freedom of other people along with their communities and livelihoods. There are such things as economic weapons of massive destruction. We have allowed them to be used against us, not just by public submission and regulatory malfeasance, but also by public subsidies, incentives, and sufferances impossible to justify.

We have failed to acknowledge this threat and to act in our own defense. As a result, our once-beautiful and bountiful countryside has long been a colony of the coal, timber, and agribusiness corporations, yielding an immense wealth of energy and raw materials at an immense cost to our land and our land's people. Because of that failure also, our towns and cities have been gutted by the likes of Wal-Mart, which have had the permitted luxury of destroying locally owned small businesses by means of volume discounts.

The Need for Protection Against Corporate Abuse

Because as individuals or even as communities we cannot protect ourselves against these aggressions, we need our state and national governments to protect us. As the poor deserve as much justice from our courts as the rich, so the small farmer and the small merchant deserve the same economic justice, the same freedom in the market, as big farmers and chain stores. They should not suffer ruin merely because their rich competitors can afford (for a while) to undersell them.

Furthermore, to permit the smaller enterprises always to be ruined by false advantages, either at home or in the global economy, is ultimately to destroy local, regional, and even national capabilities of producing vital supplies such as food and textiles. It is impossible to understand, let alone justify, a government's willingness to allow the human sources of necessary goods to be destroyed by the "freedom" of this corporate anarchy. It is equally impossible to understand how a government can permit, and even subsidize, the destruction of the land and the land's productivity. Somehow we have lost or discarded any controlling sense of the interdependence of the Earth and the human capacity to use it well. The governmental obligation to protect these economic resources, inseparably human and natural, is the same as the obligation to protect us from hunger or from foreign invaders. In result, there is no difference between a domestic threat to the sources of our life and a foreign one.

It appears that we have fallen into the habit of compromising on issues that should not, and in fact cannot, be compromised. I have an idea that a large number of us, including even a large number of politicians, believe that it is wrong to destroy the Earth. But we have powerful political opponents who insist that an Earth-destroying economy is justified by freedom and profit. And so we compromise by agreeing to permit the destruction only of parts of the Earth, or to permit the Earth to be destroyed a little at a time—like the famous three-legged pig that was too well loved to be slaughtered all at once.

The logic of this sort of compromising is clear, and it is clearly fatal. If we continue to be economically dependent on destroying parts of the Earth, then eventually we will destroy it all.

Suggestions for Doing Better

So long a complaint accumulates a debt to hope, and I would like to end with hope. To do so I need only repeat something I said at the beginning: Our destructiveness has not been, and it is not, inevitable. People who use that excuse are morally incompetent, they are cowardly, and they are lazy. Humans don't have to live by destroying the sources of their life. People can change; they can learn to do better. All of us, regardless of party, can be moved by love of our land to rise above the greed and contempt of our land's exploiters. This of course leads to practical problems, and I will offer a short list of practical suggestions.

We have got to learn better to respect ourselves and our dwelling places. We need to quit thinking of rural America as a colony. Too much of the economic history of our land has been that of the export of fuel, food, and raw materials that have been destructively and too cheaply produced. We must reaffirm the economic value of good stewardship and good work. For that we will need better accounting than we have had so far.

We need to reconsider the idea of solving our economic problems by "bringing in industry." Every state government appears to be scheming to lure in a large corporation from somewhere else by "tax incentives" and other squanderings of the people's money. We ought to suspend that practice until we are sure that in every state we have made the most and the best of what is already there. We need to build the local economies of our communities and regions by adding value to local products and marketing them locally before we seek markets elsewhere.

We need to confront honestly the issue of scale. Bigness has a charm and a drama that are seductive, especially to politicians and financiers; but bigness promotes greed, indifference, and damage, and often bigness is not necessary. You may need a large corporation to run an airline or to manufacture cars, but you don't need a large corporation to raise a chicken or a hog. You don't need a large corporation to process local food or local timber and market it locally.

And, finally, we need to give an absolute priority to caring well for our land—for every bit of it. There should be no compromise with the destruction of the land or of anything else that we cannot replace. We have been too tolerant of politicians who, entrusted with our country's defense, become the agents of our country's destroyers, compromising on its ruin.

And so I will end this by quoting my fellow Kentuckian, a great patriot and an indomitable foe of strip mining, Joe Begley of Blackey: "Compromise, hell!"

Environmental Degradation Is Fueled by Consumption

Hillary Mayell

Hillary Mayell is a reporter for National Geographic News. *In the following article, she reports on the 2004 Worldwatch Institute study that describes the devastating toll of overconsumption on the Earth's water supplies, natural resources, and ecosystems. Worldwatch claims that most of the environmental issues we see today can be linked to consumption. Climate change is directly related to the production of consumer goods, for example, and climate change is responsible for the extinction of animal species. While consumerism in the past was a feature of Western society, today it is a worldwide phenomenon, and the effects on the environment are that much greater. Unbridled consumption is already having ecological and societal repercussions, according to Worldwatch, and in order to save ourselves, humans must change the way we produce goods and the way we consume them.*

Americans and Western Europeans have had a lock on unsustainable over- consumption for decades. But now developing countries are catching up rapidly, to the detriment of the environment, health, and happiness, according to the Worldwatch Institute in its annual report, *State of the World 2004.*

Perfectly timed after the excesses of the holiday season, the report put out by the Washington, D.C.–based research organization focuses on consumerism run amuck.

Approximately 1.7 billion people worldwide now belong to the "consumer class"—the group of people characterized by diets of highly processed food, desire for bigger houses, more and bigger cars, higher levels of debt, and lifestyles devoted to the accumulation of non-essential goods.

Today nearly half of global consumers reside in developing countries, including 240 million in China and 120 million in India—markets with the most potential for expansion.

"Rising consumption has helped meet basic needs and create jobs," Christopher Flavin, president of Worldwatch Institute said in a statement to the press. "But as we enter a new century, this unprecedented consumer appetite is undermining the natural systems we all depend on, and making it even harder for the world's poor to meet their basic needs."

The report addresses the devastating toll on the Earth's water supplies, natural resources, and ecosystems exacted by a plethora of disposable cameras, plastic garbage bags, and other cheaply made goods with built in product-obsolescence, and cheaply made manufactured goods that lead to a "throw away" mentality.

"Most of the environmental issues we see today can be linked to consumption," said Gary Gardner, director of research for Worldwatch. "As just one small example, there was a story in the newspaper just the other day saying that 37 percent of species could become extinct due to climate change, which is very directly related to consumption."

From Luxuries to Necessities

Globalization is a driving factor in making goods and services previously out of reach in developing countries much more available. Items that at one point in time were considered luxuries—televisions, cell phones, computers, air conditioning—are now viewed as necessities.

China provides a snapshot of changing realities. For years, the streets of China's major cities were characterized by a virtual sea of people on bicycles, and 25 years ago there were barely any private cars in China. By 2000, 5 million cars moved people and goods; the number is expected to reach 24 million by the end of [2006].

In the United States, there are more cars on the road than licensed drivers.

Increased reliance on automobiles means more pollution, more traffic, more use of fossil fuels. Cars and other forms of transportation account for nearly 30 percent of world energy use and 95 percent of global oil consumption.

Changing diet, with a growing emphasis on meat, illustrates the environmental and societal toll exacted by unbridled consumption.

To provide enough beef, chicken, and pork to meet the demand, the livestock industry has moved to factory farming. Producing eight ounces of beef requires 6,600 gallons (25,000 liters) of water; 95 percent of world soybean crops are consumed by farm animals, and 16 percent of the world's methane, a destructive greenhouse gas, is produced by belching, flatulent livestock. The enormous quantities of manure produced at factory farms becomes toxic waste rather than fertilizer, and runoff threatens nearby streams, bays, and estuaries.

Chickens at a typical farm are kept in cages with about nine square inches (about 60 square centimeters) of space per bird. To force them to lay more eggs, they are often starved. Chickens slaughtered for meat are first fattened up with hormones, sometimes to the point where their legs can no longer support their weight.

Crowded conditions can lead to the rapid spread of disease among the animals. To prevent this, antibiotics are included in their feed. The World Health Organization reports that the widespread use of these drugs in the livestock industry is helping breed antibiotic-resistant microbes, complicating the treatment of disease in both animals and people.

Inroads are being made. In 2002, McDonald's announced it would stop buying eggs from suppliers who keep chickens confined in battery cages and that are forced to lay additional eggs through starvation. By 2004, the fast-food chain will require chicken suppliers to stop giving birds antibiotics to promote growth. Wendy's, Burger King, and Kentucky Fried Chicken have all hired animal welfare specialists to devise new animal care standards.

The World Bank has also rethought its policy of funding livestock factory farming. In 2001, a World Bank report concluded "there is a significant danger that the poor are being crowded out, the environment eroded, and global food safety and security threatened."

Not Much Happier

The increase in prosperity is not making humans happier or healthier, according to several studies. Findings from a survey of life satisfaction in more than 65 countries indicate that income and happiness tend to track well until about $13,000 of annual income per person (in 1995 dollars). After that, additional income appears to produce only modest increments in self-reported happiness.

Increased consumerism evidently comes at a steep price.

People are incurring debt and working longer hours to pay for the high-consumption lifestyle, consequently spending less time with family, friends, and community organizations.

"Excess consumption can be counterproductive," said Gardner. "The irony is that lower levels of consumption can actually cure some of these problems."

Diets of highly processed food and the sedentary lifestyle that goes with heavy reliance on automobiles have led to a worldwide epidemic of obesity. In the United States, an estimated 65 percent of adults are overweight or obese, and the country has the highest rate of obesity among teenagers in the world. Soaring rates of heart disease and diabetes, surging health care costs, and a lower quality of day-to-day life are the result.

Some aspects of rampant consumerism have resulted in startling anomalies. Worldwatch reports that worldwide annual expenditures for cosmetics total U.S. $18 billion; the estimate for annual expenditures required to eliminate hunger and malnutrition is $19 billion. Expenditures on pet food in the United States and Europe total $17 billion a year; the estimated cost of immunizing every child, providing clean drinking water for all, and achieving universal literacy is $16.3 billion.

There is, of course, no easy solution to the problem. The authors call for green taxes (to reflect the true environmental costs of a product), take-back programs that require manufacturers to recycle packaging or goods, and consumer education and awareness programs.

But first and foremost we need to reorient our way of thinking, says Gardner.

"The goal is to focus not so much on sacrifice, but on how to provide a higher quality of life using the lowest amount of raw materials," he said. "We need to change the way we produce goods and the way we consume them."

Consumerism Has Benefited the Environment

John A. Charles Jr.

John A. Charles Jr. is president and CEO of Cascade Policy Institute, a Portland, Oregon-based think tank. In the following article, first published in 2000, he argues against environmentalists who claim that the American consumer lifestyle is unsustainable and that the adoption of consumerist values by other countries would seriously deplete the world's resources. He believes that, counter to what environmentalists claim, the United States economy is now less polluting and more efficient than it was fifty years ago and that it uses less energy as well. He also maintains that some natural resources are more abundant than they were in the past and that water and air quality are better than they have ever been. He contends that limiting the entrepreneurial impulse in the name of sustainability is a mistake and that free markets are best suited to produce environmental gain.

Environmental activists who criticize free trade generally make one or both of the following arguments. First, they criticize the American lifestyle as environmentally "unsustainable" and fear that adoption of similar values by others through globalization would result in catastrophic shortages of finite natural resources. The standard summation of this concern is that if everyone in India and China lived them same resource-intensive lifestyle as the average American, we'd need "seven more earths" to provide all the natural resources.[1]

The second argument is that intentional trade agreements such as NAFTA haven't given other nations the power to invalidate U.S. environmental laws, thereby promoting a "race to the bottom" of ever-weakening regulations exploited by multinational corporations.

John A. Charles Jr., "The Environmental Benefits of Globalization," *Cascade Policy Institute*, February 2003. Reproduced by permission.

Both of these concerns can be addressed without imposing artificial barriers to trade.

Is the American Lifestyle Unsustainable?

Perhaps the most direct measure of sustainability is the amount of energy consumed per unit of economic output. If an economic system takes increasing amounts of energy over time to produce the same unit of output, then it's unlikely to sustain itself. An economy that does more with less each year is one that is likely built for the long haul.

The U.S. economy has shown a remarkable drop in energy intensity during the past 50 years. Between 1949 and 2000, energy consumption per dollar of Gross Domestic Product (GDP) dropped from 20.63 thousand Btu to 10.57. In other words, at the beginning of the new millennium, we were able to produce the same economic output that we had in 1949 using only half as much energy.

Other indicators are equally positive. Between 1970 and 1997, U.S. population increased 31 percent, vehicle miles traveled increased 127 percent, and gross domestic product increased 114 percent—yet total air pollution actually decreased by about 31 percent.

How is it that as the economy grows, pollution keeps falling? The answer is simple: market competition imposes a never-ending drive for efficiency and innovation. Since pollution results from the waste of a resource input, rising industrial efficiency results in lowered pollution.

The overall growth in living standards has had tremendous public health benefits as well. The infant mortality rate in the United States dropped from 29.2 per thousand in 1950 to 6.63 in 2006. Since 1980, the death rate for cancer has dropped more than 11% for individuals between the ages of 25 and 64.

In short, wealthier is healthier. A recent report by the World Trade Organization reinforces these points. The report concludes:

"One reason why environmental protection is lagging in many countries is low incomes. Countries that live on the margin may simply not be able to afford to set aside resources for pollution abatement. . . . If poverty is at the core of the problem, economic growth will be part of the solution, to the extent that it allows countries to shift gears from more immediate concerns to long run sustainability issues. Indeed, at least some empirical evidence suggests that pollution increases at the early stages of development but decreases after a certain income level has been reached. . . ."

The state interventionist model favored by many "sustainability" advocates has been tried numerous times and always failed. Some of the most polluted cities on the face of the earth are in countries formerly or currently under socialist rule. Leaders of the former Soviet Union and East Germany were as confident in their ability to run the economy as local sustainable development advocates are in Oregon, but they found out that eliminating market competition also eliminated incentives to develop innovative technologies that use resources more efficiently.

It's time to acknowledge that the search for a sustainable economy is over. We've already got one; we just need to protect it from the meddling of politicians and bureaucrats who simply can't stand the idea of "unplanned" voluntary trade in a free society.

Note

1. Alan Thein Durning, Northwest Environment Watch, personal communication with author, 1998.

Energy Scarcity Will Change the Way We Consume

James Howard Kunstler

James Howard Kunstler is an author and social critic best known for his book The Geography of Nowhere, *about the history of suburban and urban development in the United States. In the following article, originally delivered as a speech to the Commonwealth Club of California, he argues that the coming age of energy scarcity will change everything about how Americans live—most of all their dependency on automobiles.*

In my book *The Long Emergency* I wrote that our nation was sleepwalking into an era of unprecedented hardship and disorder—largely due to the end of reliably cheap and abundant oil. We're still blindly following that path into a dangerous future, lost in dark raptures of infotainment, diverted by inane preoccupations with sex and celebrity, made frantic by incessant motoring.

The coming age of energy scarcity will change everything about how we live in this country. It will ignite more desperate contests between nations for the remaining oil and natural gas around the world. It will alter the fundamental terms of industrial economies. It will ramify and amplify many of the problems presented by climate change. It will require us to behave differently. But we are not paying attention.

As the American public continues sleepwalking into a future of energy scarcity, climate change, and geopolitical turmoil, we have also continued dreaming. Our collective dream is one of those super-vivid ones people have just before awakening, as the fantastic transports of the unconscious begin to merge with the demands of waking reality. The dream is a

James Howard Kunstler, "We Must Imagine a Future Without Cars," *Alternet*, April 4, 2007. Reproduced by permission.

particularly American dream on an American theme: how to keep all the cars running by some other means than gasoline. *We'll run them on ethanol! We'll run them on biodiesel, on synthesized coal liquids, on hydrogen, on methane gas, on electricity, on used French-fry oil. . . !*

Dwindling Oil Supplies

The dream goes around in fevered circles as each gasoline-replacement is examined and found to be inadequate. But the wish to keep the cars going is so powerful that round and round the dream goes. *Ethanol! Biodiesel! Coal Liquids. . . .*

And a harsh reality indeed awaits us as the full scope of the permanent energy crisis unfolds. The global oil production peak is not a cult theory, it's a fact. The earth does not have a creamy nougat center of petroleum. The supply is finite, and we have ample evidence that all-time global production has peaked.

Of course, the issue is not about running out of oil, and never has been. There will always be some oil left underground—it just might take more than a barrel-of-oil's worth of energy to pump each barrel out, so it won't be worth doing.

The issue is not about running out—it's about what happens when you head over the all-time production peak down the slippery slope of depletion. And what happens is that the complex systems we depend on for everyday life in advanced societies begin to falter, wobble, and fail—and the failures in each system will in turn weaken the others. By complex systems I mean the way we produce our food, the way we conduct manufacture and trade, the way we operate banking and finance, the way we move people and things from one place to another, and the way we inhabit the landscape.

I'll try not to dwell excessively on the statistics since I am more concerned here with the implications for everyday life in our nation. But it is probably helpful to understand a few of the numbers.

Oil Production and Consumption

Oil production in the US peaked in 1970. We're now producing about half of what we did then, and our own production continues to run down steadily at the rate of a few percentage points of recoverable reserves each year. It adds up. In 1970, we were producing about 10 million barrels a day. Now we're down to less than five—and we consume over 20 million barrels a day. We have compensated for that since 1970 by importing oil from other nations. Today we import about two-thirds of all the oil we use. Today, the world is consuming all the oil it can produce. As global production passes its own peak, the world will not be able to compensate for its shortfall by importing oil from other planets.

Nor is there any real likelihood that new discoveries will be adequate to compensate. Discovery precedes production, of course, because you can't pump oil that you haven't discovered. Discovery of oil in the US peaked in the 1930s—and production started declining roughly 30 years later. Discovery of oil peaked worldwide in the 1960s, and now the signs suggest the world has peaked. Discovery of new oil worldwide in recent years has amounted to a tiny fraction of replacement levels. In fact, we may be burning more oil just in our exploration efforts than we will get from the oil we're discovering.

The oil industry has been dominated by what are called supergiant fields. The four reigning supergiant fields of oil of our time were discovered decades ago and are now in decline. The Burgan field of Kuwait, the Daqing of China, Cantarell of Mexico, and Ghawar of Saudi Arabia. Together in recent decades they were responsible for 14 percent of the world's oil production, and they are now in decline. All except Ghawar of Saudi Arabia have been declared officially past peak by their own governments and Ghawar is showing clear signs of trouble—though Aramco [the Saudi national oil company] itself won't say so. Ghawar has provided 60 percent of Saudi Arabia's production. Saudi Arabia's total production is down 8 percent in [2006], despite a massive increase in drilling rigs, and the incentive of high prices.

[In 2006], the Mexican national oil company, Pemex, declared its supergiant field, Cantarell, to be officially past peak and in decline. As in the case with Ghawar and Saudi Arabia, Cantarell has been responsible for 60 percent of Mexico's oil production. Cantarell is now crashing at an official decline rate of at least 15 percent a year—perhaps steeper. Mexico has been our No. 3 source of oil imports (after Canada and Saudi Arabia). The crash of Cantarell means in just a few years Mexico, our No. 3 source of imports, will have no surplus oil to sell to the US. It also means that the Mexican government will be strapped for operating revenue—and you can draw your own conclusions about the political implications.

The North Sea and Alaska's North Slope were some of the last great discoveries of the oil era. Plentiful North Sea and Alaskan production took away OPEC's [Organization of Petroleum Exporting Countries] leverage over the oil markets. This led to the oil glut of the 1990s, driving oil prices down finally to $10 a barrel. It is also what induced the American public to fall asleep on energy issues. It seemed as if cheap oil was here to stay. Forever.

Both The North Sea and Alaska are now past peak and in depletion. Prudhoe Bay proved to be Alaska's only super giant oil field. Several other key fields were discovered. None were even 1/6th the size of Prudhoe Bay.

North Sea oil was produced using the latest-and-greatest new technology for drilling and guess what: it only allowed the region to be drained more rapidly and efficiently. Now 57 of Norway's 69 oil fields are past peak and the average post-peak decline rates average 17 percent a year. The UK's share of the North Sea has declined to the extent that England is now a net energy importer.

Russia, despite current high levels of post-Soviet-era production, peaked in the 1980s, and may now be past 70 percent of its ultimate recoverable reserves. Iran is past peak. Indonesia, an OPEC member, is so far past peak it became a net oil importer [in 2006]. Venezuela is past peak. Iraq and Nigeria are consumed by political insurrection. The companies developing Canada's tar sands have announced that their costs will double original estimates—in other words, whatever comes out of the ground there will be very expensive.

Declining Production, Increased Consumption

Meanwhile, in the background, completely ignored by the US media, an additional problem is developing on the oil scene. Net world production is going down by just under 3 percent a year, but *total exports from the top ten exporters are going down at an even steeper rate.* Geologist Jeffrey Brown, among the excellent technicians at TheOilDrum.com website, writes that the top ten exporters are showing a net export decline rate of 7 percent the past year [2006], trending toward a 50 percent export decline over the coming ten years. Why? Because on top of production decline rates, nations like Saudi Arabia, Iran, and Venezuela are using more of their own oil at home with rising populations and more automobiles.

A few additional background items. Most of the easy-to-get, light and sweet crude oil is gone. We got that out of the ground in the run-up to peak. We found that high quality oil in temperate places onshore, like Texas, where it was easy and pleasant to work, and the stuff was relatively close to the surface. The remaining oil is, each year, proportionally made up more of heavy and sour crudes that are hard to refine and yield less gasoline. Most of the refinery capacity in the world cannot process these heavy and sour crudes and there is no world-class industrial effort to build new ones—and on top of that, existing world refinery infrastructure is old and rusty. Finally, most of the remaining oil in the world exists either in geographically forbidding places where it is extremely difficult and expensive to work, like deep water out in the ocean or in frozen regions, or else it belongs to people who are indisposed to be friendly to us.

The natural gas situation is at least equally ominous, with some differences in the technical details—and by the way, I'm referring here not to gasoline but to methane gas (CH_4), the stuff we run in kitchen stoves and home furnaces. Natural gas doesn't deplete slowly like oil, following a predictable bell curve pattern; it simply stops coming out of the ground very suddenly, and then that particular gas well is played out. You get your gas from the continent you're on. Natural gas is moved to customers in the US, Canada, and Mexico in an extensive pipeline network. To import natural gas from overseas, it has to be liquefied, loaded in a special kind of expensive-to-build-and-operate tanker ship, and then offloaded at a specialized marine terminal, all adding layers of cost. The process also obviously affords us poor control over not-always-friendly foreign suppliers.

Half the homes in America are heated with gas furnaces and about 16 percent of our electricity is made with it. Industry uses natural gas as the main ingredient in fertilizer, plastics, ink, glue, paint, laundry detergent, insect repellents and many other common household necessities. Synthetic rubber and man-made fibers like nylon could not be made without the chemicals derived from natural gas. In North America, natural gas production peaked in 1973. We are drilling as fast as we can to keep the air conditioners and furnaces running.

Suburbia Runs on Cheap Oil and Gas

That's the background on our energy predicament. Against this background is the whole question of how we live in the United States. I wrote three books previously about the fiasco of suburbia. There are many ways of describing it, but lately I refer to it as *the greatest misallocation of resources in the history of the world.* Why? Because it is a living arrangement with no future. Why doesn't it have a future? Because it was designed to run on cheap oil and gas, and in just a few years we won't have those things anymore.

Having made these choices, we are now hobbled by a tragic *psychology of previous investment*—that is, having poured so much of our late-20th century wealth into this living arrangement—this Happy Motoring utopia—we can't imagine letting go of it, or substantially reforming it.

We have compounded the problem lately by making the building of suburban sprawl the basis of our economy. Insidiously, we have replaced America's manufacturing capacity with an economy based on building ever more suburban houses and the accessories and furnishings that go with them—the highway strips, the big box shopping pods, et cetera—meaning that our economy is now largely based on building more and more stuff with no future—on a continued misallocation of resources. Roughly 40 percent of the new jobs created between 2001 and [2006] were in housing bubble related fields—the builders, the real estate agents, the mortgage brokers, the installers of granite countertops. If you subtracted the housing bubble from the rest of the economy in recent years, there wouldn't be much left besides hair-styling, fried chicken, and open heart surgery. Much of this housing bubble itself was promulgated by an equally unprecedented lapse in standards and norms of finance—a tragedy-in-the-making that has now begun to unwind. What are we going to do about our extreme oil dependence and the living arrangement that goes with it?

There's a widespread wish across America these days that some combination of alternative fuels will rescue us; will allow us to continue enjoying by some other means what has been called "the non-negotiable American way of life." The wish is perhaps understandable given the psychology of previous investment.

But the truth is that no combination of alternative fuels or systems for using them will allow us to continue running America the way we have been, or even a substantial fraction of it. We are not going to run Wal Mart, Walt Disney World, Monsanto, and the interstate highway system on any combination of solar or wind energy, hydrogen, nuclear, ethanol, tar sands, oil shale, methane hydrates, thermal depolymerization, *zero-point* energy, used french-fry oil, or anything else you can name. We will desperately use many of these things in many ways, but we are likely to be disappointed by what they can actually do for us, particularly in terms of scale—apart from the fact that most or all of them are probably net energy losers in economic terms.

For instance, we are much more likely to use wind power on a household or neighborhood basis rather than in deployments of Godzilla-sized turbines in so-called wind farms.

What We Must Do

The key to understanding what we face is that we have to comprehensively make other arrangements for all the normal activities of everyday life. It is a long, detailed "to do" list that we can't afford to ignore. The public discussion of these issues is impressively incoherent. This failure of the collective imagination is reflected in the especially poor job being done by the mainstream media covering this story—in particular, *The New York Times*, which does little besides publish feel-good press releases from Cambridge Energy Research Associates, the oil industry's chief public relations consultant.

These days, the only aspect of these issues that we are willing to talk about at all is how we might keep all our cars running by other means. We have to get beyond this obsession with running the cars by other means. The future is not just about motoring. We have to make other arrangements comprehensively for all the major activities of daily life in this nation.

We'll have to grow our food differently. The ADM/ Monsanto/Cargill model of industrial-scale agribusiness will not survive the discontinuities of the Long Emergency—the system of pouring oil-and-gas-based fertilizers and herbicides on the ground to grow all the cheez doodles and hamburgers. As oil and gas deplete, we will be left with sterile soils and farming organized at an unworkable scale. Many lives will depend on our ability to fix this.

We will find out the hard way that we can't afford to dedicate our crop lands to growing grains and soybeans for ethanol and biodiesel. A Pennsylvania farmer put it this way to me [recently]: "*It looks like we're going to take the last six inches of Midwest topsoil and burn it in our gas tanks.*" The disruptions to world grain supplies by the ethanol mania are just beginning to thunder through the system. [In March 2007] there were riots in Mexico City because so much Mexican corn is now already being diverted to American ethanol production that poor people living on the economic margins cannot afford to pay for their food staples.

You can see, by the way, how this is a tragic extension of our obsession with running all the cars.

Going Local

In the years ahead, farming will come back much closer to the center of American economic life. It will necessarily have to be done more locally, at a smaller-and-finer scale, and will require more human attention. Many of the value-added activities associated with farming—making products like cheese, wine, oils—will also have to be done much more locally. This situation presents excellent business and vocational opportunities for America's young people. It also presents huge problems in land-use reform. Not to mention the fact that the knowledge and skill for doing these things has to be painstakingly retrieved from the dumpster of history.

We're going to have to move people and things from place to place differently. It is imperative that we restore the US passenger railroad system. No other project we could do right away would have such a positive impact on our oil consumption. We used to have a railroad system that was the envy of the world. Now we have a system that the Bulgarians would be ashamed of.

The infrastructure for this great task is lying out there rusting in the rain. This project would put scores of thousands of people to work at meaningful jobs, at every level, from labor to management. It would benefit all ranks of society. Fixing the US passenger rail system doesn't require any great technological leaps into the unknown. The technology is thoroughly understood. The fact that from end-to-end of the political spectrum there is no public discussion about fixing the US passenger rail system shows how un-serious we are.

There's another compelling reason we should undertake the great project of repairing the US passenger rail system: it is something that would restore our confidence, a way we could demonstrate to ourselves that we are competent and capable of meeting the difficult challenges of this energy-scarce future. . . . And it might inspire us to get on with the other great tasks that we will have to face.

Electrifying Railroads

By the way, it is important that we electrify our railroad system. All the other advanced nations have electric rail systems which allow them to run on something other than fossil fuel or to control the source point of the carbon emissions and pollution in the case of coal-fired power generation. Electric motors are far simpler and way more efficient even than diesel engines. The US was well underway with the project of electrifying our railroad system, but we just gave up after the Second World War as we directed all our investment to the interstate highway system instead.

We're going to have to move things by boat. But we've just finished a 50-year effort in taking apart most of the infrastructure for maritime trade in America. Our harbors and riverfronts have been almost completely de-activated. The public now thinks that harbors and riverfronts should only be used for condo sites, parks, bikeways, band shells and festival marketplaces. Guess what: We're going to have to put back the piers and warehouses and even the crummy accommodations for sailors.

We're going to have to move a lot more stuff by water or our ability to do commerce will suffer. Meanwhile, if we use trucks, it will be for the very last local increment of the journey. Leaders in business and municipal politics will have to wrap their minds around this new reality.

The End of the Age of Happy Motoring

We are probably in the twilight of Happy Motoring—as we have known it. The automobile will be a diminished presence in our lives. I'm not saying that cars will disappear, but it will become self-evident that our extreme dependency will have to end. It is possible, but not likely, that affordable electric cars will come on the market before we get into serious trouble with oil. More likely, we'll be facing an entirely new political problem with cars as motoring becomes increasingly only something that the economic elite can enjoy.

For decades, motoring has been absolutely democratic. Everybody from the lowliest hamburger flipper to the richest Microsoft millionaire could participate in the American motoring program. Right now, let's say six percent of adults in this nation can't drive, for one reason or another: They're blind, too old, too poor, et cetera. What if that number rose to 13 percent, or 26 percent of Americans because either the price of fuel or the cost of a vehicle rose beyond their means. Do you suppose that a whole new mood of grievance and resentment might arise against those who were still driving cars?

And how would the large new class of non-drivers feel about paying taxes to maintain the very expensive interstate highway systems?

Back to the task list:

We're going to have to make other arrangements for commerce and manufacturing. The national chain discount stores that took over American retail in recent decades will not survive the discontinuities of the Long Emergency. Their business equations and methods of operations will fail, in particular their remorseless cancer-like drive toward replication and expansion. They will lack the resilience to adapt due to their gigantic scale of operations—a scale that will no longer be appropriate to the contracting available energy "nutrients."

The so-called "warehouse on wheels" composed of thousands of trucks circulating incessantly around the interstate highways will not work economically in a new era of scarcer and expensive oil. Not to mention the 12,000-mile supply line to the factories of Asia which we have tragically come to depend on for so many of our household goods.

We have to check all our assumptions at the door about how things will work in the years ahead. Lately, thanks to [business journalist] Tom Friedman and other cheerleaders for the global economy, we've adopted the notion that globalism is a permanent condition of life. I think we will be disappointed to learn the truth—that globalism was a set of transient economic relations made possible at a particular time by very special conditions, namely half a century of cheap energy and half a century of relative peace between the great powers.

Those conditions are about to end, and with them, I predict, will go many of the far-flung economic relations that we've come to rely on. When the US and China are contesting for the world's remaining oil resources, do you think it's possible that our trade relations might be affected? These are things we had better be prepared to think about it. China has way outstripped its own dwindling oil supply. China has gone

all over the world in recent years systematically making con-
tracts for future delivery of oil with other nations, including
Canada, as that nation ramps up production of the tar sands
in Alberta.

I want to remind you that there is such a thing as the
Monroe Doctrine, an American foreign policy position that
essentially forbids nations outside the western hemisphere
from intruding in or exploiting affairs in this part of the
world. It may be an old and perhaps an arrogant policy—but
I predict the time will come when the United States will in-
voke it in order to preserve our access to Canadian oil supplies. And if-and-when that occurs, what do you suppose that
will mean to our trade relations with China? How many plastic wading pools and salad shooters will Wal-Mart be ordering
then?

These are the kinds of things we are not thinking about at
all, and which leave us woefully unprepared to face a very uncertain future.

CHAPTER 5

Personal Perspectives on Consumerism

Kicking the Consumerism Habit Is Not Easy

Wendee Holtcamp

Wendee Holtcamp is a writer and photographer. In the following article, she describes her own personal social experiment—a thirty-day moratorium on shopping for new "stuff." She considers whether her choice to buy only used goods in fact made any important impact on the environment. Whether or not the effects of her actions made any profound ecological effects, she found that the thirty days of not buying anything new provided her with a renewed understanding of her needs versus her wants.

A few days into a vow of shopping celibacy, I visit a Hallmark store with my kids. The 75-percent-off rack draws me in. I've forgotten that I'm supposed to be living according to the Compact, an agreement to avoid all new purchases in favor of used goods in an attempt to reduce my impact on the environment.

"Look at these cute penguins," I say, showing them to my kids.

My 10-year-old son, Sam, picks one up. "Cool. They poop candy."

I pay and leave the store before realizing what I've done. I stop short. "I am not supposed to buy anything new!" I yelp. My kids glare at me. "Well," I say, taking a deep breath, "I will just have to start again tomorrow."

No New Stuff

The original Compacters, who formed their group in early 2006, did not intend to start a movement. It was just 10 San Francisco friends trying to reduce their consumption by not

Wendee Holtcamp, "My 30 Days of Consumer Celibacy," *OnEarth*, Summer 2007. Reproduced by permission.

buying new stuff for a year. The group's manifesto was simple: to counteract the negative global environmental and socioeconomic impacts of U.S. consumer culture. Named after the Pilgrims' revolutionary Mayflower Compact, the small idea led to a Yahoo Web site that has attracted more than 8,000 adherents and spawned some 50 groups in spots as far-flung as Hong Kong and Iceland.

What they don't say on the Compact Web site: Kicking consumerism may require its own 12-step program. So after my Hallmark relapse, I started again from square one. According to the guidelines, I must buy used, or borrow. No new stuff, with the exception of food, necessary medicines and health care items, and—no joke—underwear.

"This all started over a dinner conversation about the limitations of recycling," says Rachel Kesel, a professional dog walker and one of the original friends who established the Compact. What else could people do to tread more lightly on the earth? "One of the solutions is not to buy so much crap."

The average American generates about 4.5 pounds of trash a day—a figure that, according to the Environmental Protection Agency, includes paper, food, yard trimmings, furniture, and everything else you toss out at home and on the job. That makes the United States the trashiest country in the industrialized world, followed by Canada at 3.75 pounds a day and the Netherlands at 3 pounds a day. In part, we can thank the corporations that spend billions to convince us that the newest, shiniest widgets will make us happy and attract friends and lovers. What's more, each new widget is designed to wear out or otherwise fade into obsolescence, so we'll have almost no choice but to buy more and more. In the words of Dr. Seuss's Once-ler in *The Lorax*, "A Thneed's a Fine-Something-That-All-People-Need!!" The old Thneed—often in working condition—goes out with the trash. And in the process of making thneeds, the Swomee-Swans get smog in their throats and the Super-Axe-Hacker whacks all the Truffala-Trees, and the gills of the Humming-Fish get gummed up with Gluppity-Glup.

I was already an eco-savvy consumer when I began my moratorium on new stuff. I bought organic produce, "green" beauty products, compact fluorescent lightbulbs, and the like. "A month won't be too bad," I told my preteen daughter. Without thinking I added, "I'll just buy everything I need beforehand." She laughed. As if I were joking.

Criticism of "The Compact"

The Compact has, for the most part, attracted people who were already living frugally or eco-consciously and whose dismay over society's overzealous buying habits may have been brewing for some time. Such feelings are not universally shared. On a Seattle radio show that aired just after the group formed, the host ripped into John Perry, one of the original Compacting friends, saying, "You people are bad for America and you're bad for the American economy."

A Web forum mocking the Compact sprang up, one of the first posts proclaiming, "Today I'm starting a Compact wherein no one can buy anything yellow. Except bananas. And lemons. . . . Oh, wait. I need legal pads." The Compact founders were called pretentious, since they live upper-middle-class lives, and hypocritical, since one of them works in marketing—the art and science of selling goods.

After this criticism, the Compacters consulted several economists about the soundness of their premise. Alex Tabarrok, a professor of economics at George Mason University, theorizes that if throngs of citizens shopped secondhand, it would drive the market to produce higher-quality, more durable goods. Some sectors of the economy would expand, he says, as people spent more money on services or used goods, which are often sold by smaller, independent business owners. But if enough of us started buying less stuff, wouldn't corporate profits fall, leading to layoffs and a drop in the gross domestic product [GDP]—that classic index of the economy?

I ran this by Bob Costanza, a professor of ecological economics at the University of Vermont who has given some thought to the question. "If 'growing GDP' is considered to be the goal, then yes, buying secondhand will hurt 'the economy' because less stuff will be produced per unit of time," he says. "But this just shows how wrong this narrow conception of the economy is." So maybe we need to rethink the way we define a strong economy to encompass not only the health of our financial markets, but also the health of our natural resources.

Lessening the Impact

Still, not everyone immediately grasps why buying used products has less impact on the environment than buying new ones. When you buy a new widget—a cell phone, for example—the store orders a replacement, instigating a chain of events that eventually leads to more raw material being mined from the earth. In contrast, when you buy used, the seller—at a garage sale, a thrift store, or on eBay—does not put in a replacement order. The chain stops there. I nearly lost a friend once when I bought a used teak table after I had exhorted her never to buy anything that wasn't made from sustainably harvested wood. My purchase did not cause a living tree to be cut down, I told her. She didn't get it.

Giving up new stuff forced me to shop creatively. A visit to Goodwill yielded a travel mug for my Starbucks visits, clothes for my daughter, and a bongo drum to substitute for the practice pad my son needed for his drum lessons. Buying a basketball net proved more challenging. I found one through Freecycle, a Web site where users trade belongings, but it had so much rust it wouldn't have passed muster with my suburban homeowners' association. After much looking, I bought a like-new one for $30 on my local Craigslist Web site.

Then it took two weeks and 55 e-mail, text, and voice messages before I got my basketball net.

When my laptop went on the fritz, I panicked. I needed a working computer, so I went shopping for a new one. This time, the widget-maker's plan to lure me into buying the newest, shiniest model backfired. Microsoft's new Windows Vista operating system won't work with the perfectly good computer accessories I already own, so if I were to fork over a grand for a new laptop, I'd also have to buy new software, new drivers, and new Microsoft Office programs. Exasperated, I took a deep breath and went home. Sticking to my Compact vow, I hauled an old dinosaur of a computer out of the closet while I waited, impatiently, for laptop repairs.

Does It Make a Difference?

I wondered: Am I really making a difference? Do I need to eliminate *everything* I would ordinarily buy new? The answer surprised me. In *The Consumer's Guide to Effective Environmental Choices*, Michael Brower and Warren Leon of the Union of Concerned Scientists calculated the impact of various consumer purchases on four environmental problem areas: air pollution, water pollution, global warming, and habitat alteration. They analyzed the environmental footprints of everything from cheese to carpet to feminine products and then aggregated them into 50 categories of goods and services. In the end, they found that just 7 of the 50 categories were responsible for the lion's share of environmental degradation: cars and trucks; meat and poultry farming; crop production; home heating, hot water, and air conditioning; household appliances; home construction; and household water use and sewage treatment.

Interestingly, the personal items I worked so hard to forgo are not among the worst offenders. Clothing, books, magazines, and toys account for a relatively small fraction of the total environmental destruction wrought by our modern lifestyle. Brower and Leon suggest that we focus on choices that matter most: alternative energy utility providers, energy-saving appliances, organic food, and fuel-efficient or hybrid cars. Over time, buying smart may be more important than buying used.

I grew up in a log cabin with a hippie dad who chose simplicity. We had an outhouse, wood stoves, chickens, and a vegetable garden. Compacting should be second nature to me. Still, I found myself rebelling. I'm a self-employed single mom! Call me an impatient American consumer, but the truth is, I both care passionately about the environment and live in a world where I often have zero extra time. And shopping for used stuff takes *lots* of time. I made a commitment some time ago to use my purchasing power to help the environment, and spending a month Compacting forced me to reexamine my priorities. It also helped me reconsider my needs versus my wants. We could have forgone the candy-pooping penguins, and I can find many perfectly good things used—and at less cost. But eventually, I will need a brand new laptop.

"I don't think everyone has to stop shopping to change American consumption habits," Rachel Kesel tells me. "But a lot of people need to be put on detox for a while."

Freegans Make a Statement by Living Off the Waste of Millions

Becca Tucker

Becca Tucker is a reporter for Our Town, *a New York weekly. Previously she worked for the* New York Sun *and Manhattan Media. In the following essay, she describes her three days of living as a "freegan," a member of a subculture of people who make a statement by living off food and other goods that would otherwise be thrown away. For three days, Tucker joined a group of freegans in New York, dumpster-diving and foraging for food and thinking about the politics of consumption and waste.*

Day One

No coffee, no beer. The significance of those words sank in with each heavy footfall that took me past my regular Starbucks on my way to the subway.

It was only Tuesday morning, and already I was having second thoughts. Three days of eating only food recovered from the garbage might have been excessively ambitious. Two years in the city have solidified my habits into those of quite the little consumer. I could already feel a bad mood encroaching. I needed my caffeine.

But my breakfast that morning—a toasted onion bagel, a banana and a Greek yogurt, all recovered from garbage bags the night before—was a step up from my usual oatmeal. And the anticipation of the lunch I was carrying—a still-packaged Starbucks egg salad sandwich and another banana, also the products of last night's dumpster dive—sustained me, for now.

Becca Tucker, "One Person's Dumpster Is Another's Diner," *Alternet*, March 21, 2007. Reproduced by permission.

The guided "trash tour" I'd participated in the night before left no doubt that this three-day experiment was a doable feat. If I'd had more hands, I could have gathered a week's worth of food from the garbage left on the sidewalk outside D'Agostino's, three Gristedes, and a Dunkin' Donuts. (Dunkin' Donuts tosses everything every twelve hours, according to an employee.) On top of uncountable loaves of bread and bagels, leaves of lettuce and slightly brown bananas, treasures that turned up included black-and-white cookies, ginger root, beets, Lunchables, and scallion pancakes. According to Madeline Nelson, who looks like your favorite librarian and dumpster dives for most of her food, dumpstering once a week can fulfill about 85 percent of your grocery needs. Twice-weekly dives can cover 90 to 95 percent. She didn't need to come out to the trash tour, because a friend recently stayed at her apartment, and as a thank-you gift he dumpster dove her fridge stock-full.

But she was there anyway, chatting and digging, offering around the orange peppers she found, stomping her feet to stay warm. Freegans are a sociable bunch.

There is an organized group of freegans in the city, called freegan.info after its website, which draws between seven and twenty-odd members, ranging in age from teens to seventy-year-olds, to its various events. But there is no knowing how many freegans there are city-wide, or nation-wide, or world-wide, because the term freeganism is a broad belief that covers a broad range of activities. If you've found a bookshelf on the street and taken it home, well, you're sort of a freegan.

Freeganism (a conjunction of "free" and "vegan") is the philosophy that participation in our capitalist economy makes a person complicit in the exploitative practices that are used to create consumer goods. One freegan defines the term as "living beyond capitalism," which can involve any number of practices: urban foraging, hopping trains, volunteering in lieu of working a paying job, repairing things like bikes and clothes instead of buying new ones, squatting instead of paying rent.

Leia Jools, 22, does many of those things. She and her boyfriend are on a "rent strike," Jools explained as she ate blueberries out of a container from the D'Agostinos trash. In other words, they are refusing to pay to live in their Bushwick, Brooklyn apartment, a tactic that Jools predicts will work for about eight months. The last time their landlord saw them in court, she says, "he looked like he was going to cry." Jools doesn't work for a living, which leaves her plenty of time to bike around looking for promising garbage piles. She was a raw vegan for awhile, which was fortunate, since she had no gas with which to cook. Now she is paying for electricity, after a stint in the dark, because she uses her apartment to build and repair bikes as part of a freegan bike recycling workshop.

One or two of the foragers at the trash tour appeared to be homeless, and not interested in chatting (although being homeless and freegan are not mutually exclusive, as is commonly assumed). They wolfed down a sandwich or two and then wandered off into the night. But the majority were brimming with culinary gusto. Shrieks of "Mushrooms! I found mushrooms!" sent a middle-aged woman scuttling over garbage bags. When a Gristedes employee yelled somewhat disdainfully, "I hope y'all here digging through the trash have enough respect to close the bags back up, cause otherwise the rats come through!" Nelson simply reminded the group to re-tie the bags. Everyone seemed cheerfully indifferent.

Their enthusiasm made it feel natural for newcomers like me to squat on a city street and dig through garbage bags as passersby looked and looked away, but I was anxious about doing it without the strength of numbers or the help of friendly veteran guides. My worry was not about getting in trouble; dumpster diving is not illegal. It was that on my own, I might look straight-up homeless.

For self-identifying freegans, embarrassment is not an issue. "I'm not so much bound by the illusions of our culture," says Adam Weissman, 29, who does activist work twelve to sixteen hours a day for no pay and lives on $20 a week.

"Being bound by the cultural norm of whether someone's going to think it's icky or weird for me to be going through the trash is far less compelling than my sense of embarrassment or horror that I would feel for being part of the problem, by basically pumping more fuel into the economy in the form of capital, in the form of money.

"So it's not that I'm in any way not cognizant of the fact that what we're doing is socially deviant. It's quite deliberate."

But I confess that when Tuesday night rolled around, it was my fear of stigma that kept me from doing as well as I could have. I couldn't bring myself to go through bags on well-lit or well-traveled streets—even though to New Yorkers, I would hardly constitute a strange sight.

My two-hour dumpster diving tour yielded a box of frozen squash and a bag of organic lettuce from an East Village Gristedes; half a bag of organic vegan popcorn, a carrot stick and a head of broccoli from a West Village health food store called Lifethyme Natural Market; enough Dunkin' Donuts to feed an office (an entertaining thought—only telling my coworkers after the tray's been picked clean that they've just enjoyed a freegan snack); and cannoli and cookies from an East Village bakery.

Nobody stared or voiced distaste. Conversations did not hush as couples passed me with my hand deep in a mess of chopped-up produce. No one offered me a dollar.

As I pulled the beaten-up box of frozen squash out of the trash in front of Gristedes, four NYU kids walked by, guitar cases on their backs. They slowed. I tensed. "All this delicious food, just thrown away," said one. I felt my face get hot. I was surrounded by them. "Anything good?" asked another.

I stood up, ready to walk away. But there was nothing threatening in the way they were kicking at the pile of trash. They were in earnest, I realized. "Mostly just bags of lettuce, and I found some frozen squash," I answered, my temperature returning to normal.

"Eh," the first one shrugged. "Not worth dumpstering."

Day Two

Caffeine withdrawal feels like an elephant sitting on your head.

So when my friend told me that she was about to clear her freezer out, I perked up. One of her roommates recently moved out, and apparently left behind a menagerie of comestibles, including bags upon bags of gourmet coffee. It was all headed for the trash, she said, unless I wanted to dumpster dive my way through their freezer.

I thought about it for a minute. Would that be a cop-out?

Hell no. Freegans are all about a "gift economy." They organize free food markets and clothing swaps. They believe in sharing and cooperation, and, of course, diverting waste from the landfill. Besides, I wasn't sure I could muster the energy to write anything worth reading in my half-awake state.

So I supplemented my rather meager coffers from the night before with dozens of frozen hot dogs, frozen corn, and best of all, four bags of coffee.

I broke out the coffee maker at work, and by the end of the day I was all hopped up, ready to rescue overstock and scoff at expiration dates. I was doubly optimistic because this time around, I would have a guide: an East Village freegan named Harmony, 21, had offered to show me the ropes.

Harmony and I made a killing. We even stopped at some of the same places I'd gone on my own the night before—the same Gristedes and that Lifethyme Market I'd stumbled upon—but Harmony's deft, methodical persistence left no promising bag unopened (until we had filled our shopping bags and our bellies, and started getting really picky). Where I found a knot too hard to untie, or a double bag too annoying to bother with, she found cereal, kitty litter, wrapped cinnamon buns, kale, brown rice and breaded tofu from a hot buffet, and her version of gold: avocadoes.

"Are you the freegans I've been hearing about?" a woman asked eagerly as she passed us on 6th Avenue. "Well, it's nice to see you!"

By the time we reached Harmony's favorite dumpstering spot, a Food Emporium in the West Village, I had already stuffed myself and gathered more than enough for the last day of my freegan diet. My bag was exploding and my interest in foraging had dwindled to the point where I was mostly content to watch as Harmony foraged. She could just as easily be transported back a thousand years to hunter-gatherer times and placed in a thicket instead of a pile of garbage, I thought as I munched on the spine of a pineapple, enjoying the taste of Maui while standing in a pile of garbage on a dark, slushy New York City street.

When we started for home, I was limping under the weight of my bounty. The bottom of my plastic bag was about to give. Two big eggplants and a tomato rolled out of Harmony's bag onto a drainage grate while we waited for a light. The tomato was expendable, but after deliberating, she decided she'd wash and bake the eggplants. It seemed such a shame to let them go to waste, again.

Day Three

When I started this experiment I had little interest in the politics of waste. I simply wanted to see whether a person could actually eat for free in a city where a sandwich costs $7. How freeing that would be, in a way. How strange an inversion of everything that drives us to go to work every day. We have to earn, we think, because we have to eat.

But after awhile, my exuberance at opening a bag to find it full of still-warm chocolate munchkins, or a hundred fat New York-quality bagels, or fifty plastic containers of organic lettuce from Mexico, or ten wrapped and ready-to-eat sandwiches, or two dozen firm, colorful peppers, was nudged out by dismay.

Dismay is the point. It's why the freegans are here, and not on some commune upstate. "I honestly can't think of a better place for me to be, and for us to be," Weissman said in an interview. He was wearing an eggplant-colored sweater that recalled the late eighties and navy pants that seemed to be part of an MTA [Metropolitan Transit Authority] worker's uniform. Like all his clothes, and all his food, this outfit had come from the trash.

"New York is in so many ways the global mecca of the marketing of capitalism, of the marketing of consumption, of the glorification of financial industries through Wall Street. It's so much the heart of global capitalism, I think it's absolutely vital for there to be a voice in this place . . . to really say, we don't need to live this way, and in fact, the effects of this kind of living is really destroying the future for life on this planet, and at the same time, causing intense misery around the world."

Weissman had given a similar speech during the trash tour on Monday night, holding up a yogurt with a foil lid and detailing the casualties that marked its journey from a mine in Colombia to D'Agostino's. I had jotted down words in the margin of my notebook: "strip mines," "oil," "Colombian Civil War," "exploited," "farm workers," "product of carnage."

I wasn't listening. It was too distant to mean anything. The numbers, too, are beyond comprehension. So 5.4 billion pounds of food were lost at the retail level in 1995. So half the food produced in this country never gets eaten. I was more interested in the yogurt in his hand.

But now that I've had to throw away good food I've foraged from the trash to make room in the fridge for even better food, now that I've passed up wrapped cinnamon buns not because they're stale, but because there are fifty of them, it's started to sink in.

This happens every night all over the city, and to varying degrees, in every city across the country. All the energy that went into growing, producing, packaging, shipping, refrigerating, and dumping all this food is worth less than what it would cost a store to run out of something and fail to make a sale. So they deliberately overstock. And while the food and packaging gets dumped in landfills, people are going hungry just blocks away.

It's depressing. It's shameful.

It's delicious.

A Green Alternative to Consumerism

Sian Berry

Sian Berry believes that the consumer culture surrounding Christmas promotes waste and can overshadow the positive aspects of the holiday. In the following viewpoint, she discusses ways in which one can enjoy holiday gift-giving and parties without the waste and environmental damage that comes with typical Christmas shopping. Berry is a writer, activist, and politician. In 2008 she was the Green Party candidate for mayor of London.

It's far too early to start talking about Christmas, but I'm afraid I have no choice. Improbably snow-bound English villages, 'seasonal' recipes for prawns and this year's must-have gadgets, are cluttering up every [advertising] break. So, as I too have already been out recording 'Green Christmas' specials for the TV, and have been doing my research, I thought I would strike back early too.

Christmas, like the average wedding, is becoming more elaborate each year. What started out as a simple trip to church and a big meal now lasts about nine weeks and involves buying more and more every year.

It's impossible to avoid taking part, because everything to do with the Christmas season, no matter how newly invented, becomes instantly 'traditional'. Secret santas, Harry Potter films, East Enders, chocolate fountains. All suddenly compulsory as if they had been around forever. And yes, what about those king prawns? Since when were tropical crustaceans a staple part of midwinter cuisine?

Believe it or not, I do love Christmas. It's the only time of the year where my voicemail and inbox calm down and I can

Sian Berry, "Christmas Prawns? No Thanks," *New Stateman*, November 19, 2007. Copyright © 2007 *New Statesman*, Ltd. Reproduced by permission.

spend a few days eating, drinking and playing board games with my sisters and family without a bulging 'to do' list nagging at the back of my mind. At its simplest as a family get-together, Christmas is a joy, but it's so easy to let things get out of hand during the run-in and be swept away in a consumer frenzy that—needless to say—can have a terrible effect on the planet.

It's not energy use that soars at Christmas (in fact with us all staying in and drinking egg-nog, the roads are unusually quiet, and sharing the cooking has its energy plus points too) but the quantity of stuff that gets bought, wrapped, cooked and then simply wasted. Each of us receives around €90 [US$130] worth of unwanted presents each year, and over a third of the food we buy is thrown away uneaten by twelfth night [January 5].

Reduce Christmas Waste

So, with my bah-humbug detector turned up to maximum, here are my green ideas for a better Christmas, with more fun, less stress and less waste.

An easy one to start off with: buy nothing this Saturday [after U.S. Thanksgiving: annual "Buy Nothing Day"]. Yes, for twenty-four hours take a break from shopping, put that Christmas list aside, take your life back and buy nothing at all in a celebration of non-consumerism.

An ideal day to spend in front of the TV, scorning [advertisements] featuring Jamie Oliver or the Spice Girls, or at the pub with your mates talking rubbish. (I haven't checked the small print, but I think the rules of Buy Nothing Day may exempt purchases at the bar.)

Next, food. A typical Christmas dinner these days can contain ingredients that have been transported over 30,000 miles, but it's really easy to cut this down simply by picking local products off the shelf instead of far-flung alternatives: hazels rather than brazil nuts, English beer rather than Australian wine, local ham instead of Indonesian prawns.

The original midwinter festival involved a feast of seasonal produce, embellished with preserved items from earlier in the year, so root vegetables, cabbages, sprouts, dried fruit, nuts, local cheeses and chutneys are all real traditional low-carbon fare.

Don't get hormone-stuffed, frightened food for your roast, invest in an organic, free-range bird from nearby, and 'offset' the extra cost by getting a smaller one. It'll taste so much better and, with fewer grotty [unusable] bits, you won't have to worry about forcing leftovers down your relatives.

Visit your local market for a real bargain on the rest of the meal, compared with overpriced supermarket vegetables. You'll be supporting your local economy, plus, if it's unpackaged, you can buy just the amount you need and won't end up throwing half of it away.

Gift Overload and What to Do About It

Moving on to presents, as we must. Let's start by ruling out pointless gadgets that will simply end up in the cupboard after a couple of weeks. No golf ball polishers, no coffee machines that need an endless supply of little plastic cartridges, no choppers, heaters or mixers that can only do one thing—no attic fodder at all.

Instead, get non-material gifts: something useful like tickets to an event, vouchers for meals, downloads or books, or membership of an organization. . . .

If you feel obliged to get something that won't fit in an envelope, use gift-giving as an excuse to introduce your friends and family to green stuff. Basics that everyone needs are best. Get bamboo t-shirts, hemp socks, quality recycled notebooks, local organic foodstuffs or non-polluting shower gel, and make sure they know where to buy replacements when they find they love them and want more.

At the end of the season, make sure everything is recycled. We create three million tonnes of extra waste over the Christmas period and use over 250,000 trees' worth of wrapping paper, so buying recycled and putting everything from the Christmas tree to your sprout peelings in the recycling box or the compost bin is essential.

So, there's my very brief seasonal tips and the bah-humbug detector has hardly flinched. I hope this shows that having a 'perfect' Christmas doesn't involve going crazy and consuming everything in sight, and that having a 'green' Christmas doesn't involve shivering around a candle in fingerless gloves for a fortnight [two weeks]. Just don't forget to shun those prawns!

A Buddhist Perspective on Consumerism

Judith Simmer Brown

Judith Simmer Brown is a Buddhist scholar and professor of religious studies at Naropa University in Colorado. In the following article, first published in 2002, she laments the poverty and destitution in the world today and fears it will only get worse. Fueling the world's suffering, she says, is the rampant consumerism in the United States, where people daily consume 120 pounds in goods that strip the Earth of its resources. Consumerism is now infecting countries around the world, and Brown believes that Buddhism has unique insights that can respond to the suffering and stem the tide of overconsumption. But, she contends, the answer to the problem is not spiritual materialism, which can lead to people putting on psychological armor to protect themselves from the threats of life—and commodifying Buddhism itself. Rather, the key to addressing the problem of consumerism is to practice generosity, something that flies in the face of American acquisitiveness and individualism but that she believes can help people overcome their materialism and self-absorption.

Western Buddhism must serve the world, not itself. It must become, as the seventh century Indian master Shantideva wrote, the doctor and the nurse for all sick beings in the world until everyone is healed; a rain of food and drink, an inexhaustible treasure for those who are poor and destitute. We can only imagine the kinds of suffering our children will encounter. Even now, we see the poor with not enough food and no access to clean drinking water; we see ethnic and religious prejudice that would extinguish those who are different; we see the sick and infirm who have no medicine or care; we see rampant exploitation of the many for the pleasure and comfort of the few; we see the demonization of those who would challenge the reign of wealth, power, and privilege. And we know the twenty-first century will yield burgeoning populations with an ever-decreasing store of resources to nourish them.

Fueling the suffering is the relentless consumerism which pervades our society and the world. Greed drives so many of the damaging systems of our planet. The socially engaged biologist Stephanie Kaza said that in America each of us consumes our body weight each day in materials extracted and processed from farms, mines, rangelands, and forests—120 pounds on the average. Since 1950, consumption of energy, meat, and lumber has doubled; use of plastic has increased five-fold; use of aluminum has increased seventy-fold; and airplane mileage has increased thirty-three-fold per person. We now own twice as many cars as in 1950. And with every bite, every press of the accelerator, every swipe of the credit card in our shopping malls, we leave a larger ecological footprint on the face of the world. We have squeezed our wealth out of the bodies of plantation workers in Thailand, farmers in Ecuador, and factory workers in Malaysia.

The crisis of consumerism is infecting every culture of the world, most of which are now emulating the American lifestyle. David Loy, in *The Religion of the Market*, suggests that consumerism is based on two unexamined tenets or beliefs:

1. 1—growth and enhanced world trade will benefit everyone, and

2. 2—growth will not be constrained by the inherent limits of a finite planet.

The ground of consumerism is ego gratification, its path is an ever-increasing array of wants, and its fruition is expressed in the Cartesian perversion—"I shop, therefore I am." While it recruits new converts through the flood of mass media, it dulls the consumer, making us oblivious to the suffering in which we participate. Shopping is a core activity in sustaining a culture of denial.

With the collapse of communist countries throughout the world, the growth of consumerism is all but unchallenged. As traditional societies modernize, consumerism is the most alluring path. Religious peoples and communities have the power to bring the only remaining challenge to consumerism. And Buddhism has unique insights which can stem the tide of consumptive intoxication.

How do we respond to all the suffering created by consumerism? How will our children respond? It is easy to join the delusion, forgetting whatever Buddhist training we may have had. But when we return to it, we remember—the origin of suffering is our constant craving. We want, therefore we consume; we want, therefore we suffer. As practitioners, we feel this relentless rhythm in our bones. We must, in this generation, wake up to the threat of consumerism, and join with other religious peoples to find a way to break its grip. We must all find a way to become activists in the movement which explores alternatives to consumerism.

As Western Buddhists, we must recognize the threats of consumerism within our practice, and within our embryonic communities and institutions. From a Tibetan Buddhist point of view, consumerism is just the tip of the iceberg. It represents only the outer manifestation of craving and acquisitiveness. Twenty-five years ago, my guru, the Vidyadhara Chogyam Trungpa Rinpoche, wrote one of the first popular Dharma books in America, *Cutting Through Spiritual Materialism*. Its relevance only increases each year. He spoke of three levels of materialism—physical, psychological, spiritual—that rule our existence as expressions of ego-centered activity. Unchallenged, materialism will co-opt our physical lives, our communities, and our very practice.

Physical materialism refers to the neurotic pursuit of pleasure, comfort, and security. This is the outer expression of consumerism. Under this influence, we try to shield ourselves from the daily pain of embodied existence, while accentuating the pleasurable moments. We are driven to create the illusion of a pain-free life, full of choices that make us feel in control. We need 107 choices of yogurt in a supermarket so that we feel like queens of our universe. We go to 24-Plex movie theaters so that we can see whatever film we want, whenever we want. We need faster pain relievers, appliances to take away all inconvenience, and communication devices to foster immediate exchange. All of these create the illusion of complete pleasure at out fingertips, with none of the hassle of pain. When we are ruled by this kind of physical materialism, we identify ourselves by what we have.

But this is just the beginning. On the next level, psychological materialism seeks to control the world through theory, ideology, and intellect. Not only are we trying to physically manipulate the world so that we don't have to experience pain, we do so psychologically as well. We create a theoretical construct that keeps us from having to be threatened, to be wrong, or to be confused. We always put ourselves in control in this way: "As an American I have rights. As a woman, I deserve to be independent from expectations of men in my society. I earn my own salary, I can choose how I want to spend it. As a Buddhist, I understand interdependence."

Psychological materialism interprets whatever is threatening or irritating as an enemy. Then, we control the threat by creating an ideology or religion in which we are victorious, correct, or righteous; we never directly experience the fear and confusion that could arise from facing a genuine threat. This is particularly perilous for the Western Buddhist. In these times, Buddhism has become popular, a commodity which is used by corporations and the media. Being Buddhist has become a status symbol, connoting power, prestige, and money.

His Holiness's picture appears on the sets of Hollywood movies and in Apple Computer ads; Hollywood stars are pursued as acquisitions in a kind of Dharmic competition. Everyone wants to add something Buddhist to her resume. Buddhist Studies enrollments at Naropa have doubled in two years, and reporters haunt our hallways and classrooms. Buddhist conferences attract a veritable parade of characters like myself, hawking the "tools" of our trade. Our consumer society is turning Buddhism into a commodity like everything else. The seductions for the Western Buddhist are clear. We are being seduced to use Buddhism to promote our own egos, communities, and agendas in the marketplace.

This still is not the heart of the matter. On the most subtle level, spiritual materialism carries this power struggle into the realm of our own minds, into our own meditation practice. Our consciousness is attempting to remain in control, to maintain a centralized awareness. Through this, ego uses even spirituality to shield itself from fear and insecurity. Our meditation practice can be used to retreat from the ambiguity and intensity of daily encounters; our compassion practices can be used to manipulate the sheer agony of things falling apart. We develop an investment in ourselves as Buddhist practitioners, and in so doing protect ourselves from the directness and intimacy of our own realization. It is important for us to be willing to cultivate the "edge" of our own practice, the edge where panic arises, were threat is our friend, and where our depths are turned inside out.

What happens when we are ruled by the "three levels of materialism"? The Vidyadhara taught that when we are so preoccupied with issues of ego, control, and power we become "afraid of external phenomena, which are our own projections." What this means is that when we take ourselves to be real, existent beings, then we mistake the world around us to be independent and real. And when we do this we invite paranoia, fear, and panic. We are afraid of not being able to control the situation. As Patrul Rinpoche (1808–1887) taught:

Don't prolong the past,

Don't invite the future,

Don't alter your innate wakefulness,

Don't fear appearances.

We must give up the fear of appearances. How can we do this? The only way to cut this pattern of acquisitiveness and control is to guard the naked integrity of our meditation practice. We must be willing to truly "let go" in our practice. When we see our racing minds, our churning emotions and constant plots, we touch the face of the suffering world and we have no choice but to be changed. We must allow our hearts to break with the pain of constant struggle that we experience in ourselves and in the world around us. Then we can become engaged in the world, and dedicate ourselves to a genuine enlightened society in which consumerism has no sway. Craving comes from the speed of our minds, wishing so intensely for what we do not have that we cannot experience what is there, right before us.

How can we, right now, address materialism in our practice and our lives? I would like to suggest a socially engaged practice which could transform our immediate lifestyles and change our relationship with suffering. It is the practice of generosity. No practice flies more directly in the face of American acquisitiveness and individualism. Any of us who have spent time in Asia or with our Asian teachers see the centrality of generosity in Buddhist practice.

According to traditional formulation, our giving begins with material gifts and extends to gifts of fearlessness and Dharma. Generosity is the virtue that produces peace, as the sutras [Buddhist scriptures] say. Generosity is a practice which overcomes our acquisitiveness and self-absorption, and which benefits others. Committing to this practice may produce our greatest legacy for the twenty-first century.

Organizations to Contact

The editors have compiled the following list of organizations concerned with the issues presented in this book. The descriptions are derived from materials provided by the organizations. The list was compiled on the date of publication of the present volume; the information provided here may change. Be aware that many organizations take several weeks or longer to respond to inquiries, so allow as much time as possible.

Adbusters
1243 W. Seventh Ave., Vancouver, BC V6H 1B7   Canada
(604) 736-9401 • fax: (604) 737-6021
Web site: www.adbusters.org

Adbusters is a global network of artists, activists, writers, pranksters, students, educators, and entrepreneurs whose aim is to advance the new social activist movement of the information age. They declare that they seek to topple existing power structures and forge a major shift in the way humans live in the twenty-first century. To this end, Adbusters Media Foundation publishes *Adbusters* magazine, operates a Web site, and offers its creative services through PowerShift, their advocacy advertising agency. Adbusters promotes Buy Nothing Day, an informal day of protest against consumerism.

Center for a New American Dream
6930 Carroll Ave., Suite 900, Takoma Park, MD   20912
(301) 891-3683
Web site: www.newdream.org

The Center for a New American Dream helps individuals and institutions reduce and shift consumption to enhance quality of life, protect the environment, and promote social justice. Its ultimate aim is to organize enough individuals, organizations, government agencies, and companies to secure significant positive changes in the way goods are produced and consumed. The center's programs are designed to build a powerful network of individuals and institutions capable of moving from education to action on consumption issues.

Consumers Union (CU)

101 Truman Ave., Yonkers, NY   10703-1057
(914) 378-2000
Web site: www.consumersunion.org

Consumers Union is an independent, nonprofit organization dedicated to working for a fair, just, and safe marketplace for all consumers. The organization strives to change legislation and the marketplace to favor the consumer interest. CU publishes *Consumer Reports* in addition to two newsletters, *Consumer Reports on Health* and *Consumer Reports Money Advisor*.

The E. F. Schumacher Society

140 Jug End Rd., Great Barrington, MA   01230
(413) 528-1737 • fax: (413) 528-4472
Web site: www.smallisbeautiful.org

The E. F. Schumacher Society, named after the author of *Small Is Beautiful: Economics as If People Mattered,* is a nonprofit educational organization founded in 1980. Its programs demonstrate that both social and environmental sustainability can be achieved by applying the values of human-scale communities and respect for the natural environment to economic issues. Building on a tradition often known as decentralism, the society initiates practical measures that lead to community revitalization and further the transition toward an economically and ecologically sustainable society.

Ethical Consumer Research Association

41 Old Birley St., Unit 21, Manchester   M15 5RF   UK
+44 161 226 2929 • fax: +44 161 226 6277
Web site: www.ethicalconsumer.org

Ethical Consumer Research Association is a nonprofit organization owned and managed by its staff as a worker-owned cooperative. The organization researches and publishes information on companies and their products in order to promote universal human rights, environmental sustainability, and animal welfare. It publishes *Ethical Consumer Magazine*, the United Kingdom's leading alternative consumer magazine.

Freegan.info
PO Box 344, New York, NY   10108
Web site: http://freegan.info

Freegan.info is a project of the Activism Center at Wetlands Preserve, a volunteer-run, New York City-based grassroots activist collective. The organization is committed to freeganism and promotes its practice on its Web site. It discusses freegan practices, offers information for newcomers, and provides tips on dumpster diving for other freegans. It also provides numerous articles about the philosophy of freeganism, personal stories, and links to other freegan Web sites.

Make Affluence History
Web site: www.globalaware.net/affluence

This is an online group that urges affluent citizens of the world to consume less. Make Affluence History asserts that the problem of affluence is the central factor behind the structural and systematic inequalities that characterize today's global society. The group raises awareness through the sharing and distribution of educational materials, which are included on its Web site.

Overcoming Consumerism
Web site: www.verdant.net

Overcoming Consumerism is an in-depth Web site elaborating effective methods to work as an activist through everyday financial transactions. The site says that it details ways people can help defeat consumerism, save money, work less, and lead more satisfying and environmentally benign lives while help-ing to restore the economic self-sufficiency of human commu-nities. It also presents resources that can help the reader be-come a better-educated citizen and grassroots activist starting from any level of commitment and knowledge.

Redefining Progress

1904 Franklin St., Suite 600, Oakland, CA   94612
(510) 444-3041 • fax: (510) 444-3191
Web site: www.rprogress.org

Redefining Progress is a public policy think tank dedicated to finding solutions that ensure a sustainable and equitable world for future generations. While conventional models for eco-nomic growth discount such assets as clean air, safe streets, and cohesive communities, Redefining Progress integrates these assets into a more sustainable economic model. Working with government and advocacy groups, Redefining Progress develops innovative policies that balance economic well-being, environmental preservation, and social justice. Its policy ini-tiatives address pressing environmental issues such as global climate change and natural resource depletion while ensuring that both the burdens and the benefits of these policies are shared equally among affected communities.

The Simple Living Network

Web site: www.simpleliving.net/main

The Simple Living Network is a small grass-roots online ser-vice that, since 1996, has been providing resources, tools, ex-amples, and contacts for those wanting to learn how to live a more conscious, simple, healthy, and restorative lifestyle. Its goal is to present alternatives to the standard American Dream of "more . . . faster . . . bigger . . . better . . ."

Worldwatch Institute

1776 Massachusetts Ave. NW, Washington, DC   20036-1904
(202) 452-1999 • fax: (202) 296-7365
Web site: www.worldwatch.org

The Worldwatch Institute offers a blend of interdisciplinary research, global focus, and accessible writing that has made it a source of information on the interactions among key environmental, social, and economic trends. Its work revolves around the transition to an environmentally sustainable and socially just society—and how to achieve it. Its publications include the journal *World Watch* and an annual "State of the World" report. The focus of the 2004 report was "The Consumer Society."

Bibliography

Books

Allan Hunt Badiner   *Mindfulness in the Marketplace: Compassionate Responses to Consumerism.* Berkeley, CA: Parallax, 2002.

Zygmunt Bauman   *Work, Consumerism and the New Poor.* Berkshire, UK: Open University Press, 2004.

Sharon Boden   *Consumerism, Romance and the Wedding Experience.* Basingstoke, UK: Palgrave Macmillan, 2003.

Colin Campbell   *The Romantic Ethic and the Spirit of Modern Consumerism.* London: Writersprintshop, 2005.

Al Gore   *The Assault on Reason.* New York: Penguin, 2007.

Al Gore   *An Inconvenient Truth.* Emmaus, PA: Rodale, 2006.

Neva Goodwin, Frank Ackerman, and David Kiron, eds.   *The Consumer Society.* Washington, DC: Island, 1997.

Andrew Heath and Joseph Potter   *The Rebel Sell: Why Culture Can't Be Jammed.* Toronto: HarperCollins Canada, 2005.

N. Hertz — *Silent Takeover: Global Capitalism and the Death of Democracy*. London: Arrow, 2002.

Tim Jackson — *The Earthscan Reader on Sustainable Consumption*. London: Earthscan, 2006.

Tim Kasser — *The High Price of Materialism*. Boston: MIT Press, 2003.

Stephanie Kaza — *Hooked! Buddhist Writings on Greed, Desire, and the Urge to Consume*. Boston: Shambhala, 2005.

Naomi Klein — *No Logo: No Space, No Choice, No Jobs*. New York: Picador, 2002.

Kalle Lasn — *Culture Jam: How to Reverse America's Suicidal Consumer Binge—and Why We Must*. New York: HarperCollins, 2000.

Steven Miles — *Consumerism as a Way of Life*. Thousand Oaks, CA: Sage, 1998.

Richard Robbins — *Global Problems and the Culture of Capitalism*. 4th ed. Boston: Allyn & Bacon, 2007.

Juliet B. Schor — *The Overspent American: Why We Want What We Don't Need*. New York: HarperCollins, 1999.

Barry Schwartz — *The Paradox of Choice: Why More Is Less*. New York: Ecco, 2003.

Vandana Shiva   *Earth Democracy: Justice, Sustainability, and Peace.* Cambridge, MA: South End, 2005.

Marita Sturken   *Tourists of History: Memory, Kitsch, and Consumerism from Oklahoma City to Ground Zero.* Durham, NC: Duke University Press, 2007.

Pekka Sulkunen, John Holmwood, Hilary Radner, and Gerhard Schulze   *Constructing the New Consumer Society.* Basingstoke, UK: Palgrave Macmillan, 1997.

S. Thompson   *Consuming China: Approaches to Cultural Change in Contemporary China.* New York: Routledge, 2006.

Periodicals

Oliver Broudy   "Are We Doomed?" *Salon,* January 8, 2005.

Tom Carson   "Material Girl," *Atlantic Monthly,* October 2003.

Pema Chödrön   "How We Get Hooked, How We Get Unhooked," *Shambhala Sun,* March 2003.

Jared Diamond   "What's Your Consumption Factor?" *New York Times,* January 2, 2008.

Gregg Easterbrook   "The Moral Flaws of Al Gore's *An Inconvenient Truth,*" *Slate,* May 24, 2006.

Ian Frazier	"All-Consuming Patriotism," *Mother-Jones*, March-April 2002.
Michael Huesemann	"Can Pollution Problems Be Effectively Solved by Environmental Science and Technology? An Analysis of Critical Limitations," *Ecological Economics*, vol. 37, 2001.
James Kanter	"Despite Warnings, Oil Usage Expected to Increase," *International Herald Tribune*, July 9, 2007.
Carrie Lukas	"A Discount Cornucopia of Gratitude: Giving Thanks for Wal-Mart," *National Review*, November 23, 2005.
Jerry Mander and John Cavanagh	"Beyond Green Shopping," *Nation*, September 24, 2007.
Gavin McNett	"The Free Market or Your Soul," *Salon*, June 29, 1999.
Katha Pollitt	"Who Needs Christmas? They Do!" *Nation*, December 29, 2003.
Anita Purcell-Sjoelund	"Rich World's Consumerism May Cause African Famines, Experts Warn," *Agence France Presse*, July 1, 2007.
Sakyong Mipham Rinpoche	"A Reign of Goodness," *Shambhala Sun*, September 2005.
Jonathan Schroeder and Janet Borgerson	"Ethics of Consumption: The Good Life, Justice and Global Stewardship," *Journal of Consumer Affairs*, December 22, 2001.

Index